W9-CDS-978

THE LOVE OF LIBERTY

OTHER BOOKS BY LEONARD E. READ

Romance of Reality (o.p.)
Pattern for Revolt
Instead of Violence
Outlook for Freedom (o.p.)
Government: An Ideal Concept
  Governo Um Concito Ideal
Why Not Try Freedom?
  ¿Por Que No Ensayar la Libertad?
Elements of Libertarian Leadership
Anything That's Peaceful
  Todo Por la Paz
The Free Market and Its Enemy
  El Enemigo del Mercado Libre
Deeper Than You Think
Accent on the Right
The Coming Aristocracy
Let Freedom Reign
Talking to Myself
Then Truth Will Out
To Free or Freeze
Who's Listening?
Having My Way
Castles In The Air

LEONARD E. READ

THE LOVE OF LIBERTY

The Foundation for Economic Education, Inc.
Irvington-on-Hudson, New York 10533
1975

THE AUTHOR AND PUBLISHER

Leonard E. Read has been president of The Foundation for Economic Education since it was organized in 1946.

The Foundation is a nonpolitical, nonprofit, educational institution. Its senior staff and numerous writers are students as well as teachers of the free market, private ownership, limited government rationale. Sample copies of the Foundation's monthly study journal, *The Freeman,* are available on request.

Published October 1975

ISBN-O-910614-54-7

Printed in U.S.A.

To
Henry Hazlitt
who loves liberty.

God grants liberty only to those who love it, and are always ready to guard and defend it.

—Daniel Webster

The inescapable price of liberty is an *ability* to preserve it from destruction.

—General Douglas MacArthur

Those who would give up essential liberty to purchase a little temporary safety, deserve neither liberty nor safety.

—Benjamin Franklin

Liberty is the only thing you cannot have unless you are willing to give it to others.

—William Allen White

Reason and virtue alone can bestow liberty.

—Anthony A. C. Shaftesbury

With some the word liberty may mean for each man to do as he pleases with himself, and the product of his labor; while with others the same word may mean for some men to do as they please with other men, and the product of other men's labor.

—Abraham Lincoln

CONTENTS

1

THE LOVE OF LIBERTY

The love of liberty is no less imperishable than the love of knowledge.

—**FAUSTINO BALLVÉ**

My purpose here is to examine the following assumptions:

1. Liberty is impossible unless we know what it is.
2. Liberty is impossible *without* limited government.
3. Liberty is impossible *with* unlimited government.
4. Everyone loves liberty, so let's clear the decks—make it possible!

Is there knowledge of what liberty is? On the part of a few, yes; the multitude, no!

Merely take stock of what's going on now, when we "celebrate" the Bicentennial, as compared to 200 years ago when the Second Continental Congress adopted the Declaration of Independence—signed by fifty-six intrepid statesmen.[1] No other political document in history can approach our

[1]Why intrepid? For the answer, see "Would You Have Signed It?" by historian Ralph Bradford (*The Freeman*, September 1958).

Declaration as the fountainhead of liberty. Yet, at the time, the detractors were as common as the initiators were rare—the multitude and the exceptional few!

Today's situation is no different; percentage-wise, there appears to be little if any change. It's still a thousand-to-one, as we say. True, now and then there will be a Bicentennial observation portraying and highlighting precisely what our Founding Fathers had in mind. But, for the most part, the popularity of the occasion will be seized upon to bow to the shadow while trampling the very substance of liberty. From many classrooms, pulpits, political platforms, and gatherings of all kinds will flow evidence of the meager knowledge of what liberty is. For instance, it will be shouted (but not in these terms) that liberty is a liberality with the lives and livelihood of others for self-benefit. But first, what about limited and unlimited government?

Why is liberty impossible *without* limited government?

Man differs from other forms of life in that he is at once an individualistic and a social being. He resembles neither the lone eagle nor a swarm of bees. Man is both independent and interdependent.

All human beings are individualistic—independent—in the sense that each is unique in every conceivable way; no two are alike in skills, talents, aspirations, intelligence, or in any other respect. Because of your and my uniqueness, along with our extreme limitations, neither of us could live on this earth alone. Nor could anyone else! Imagine sustaining life by no more than writing or preaching or driving a truck or by any other specialization!

All human beings are dependent on others, which is to say that we are interdependent. We are all dependent upon the free, uninhibited exchanges of our numerous specializations. Thus, it should be self-evident that human survival depends on trading. We trade or perish!

The social side of man, as distinguished from the individualistic, has its origin in trading, that is, in our varied relationships with each other—economic and moral. The millions who trade—society—must, to avoid disaster, be fair and honest. Chicanery, falsehood, misrepresentation, cheating, all coercive tactics, unintelligent interpretations of self-interest must, if liberty is to prevail, be effectively restrained, inhibited. The taboos must be codified and enforced.

This necessary code is not one to be designed and enforced by any independent, unique individual—everyone doing as I say, no matter how "smart" I may be relative to others. Suppose a constabulary were to force the millions to follow me. Liberty? Unimaginable! As Caleb Colton wrote, "No man is wise enough, nor good enough, to be trusted with unlimited powers."[2] And I would add, nor is any combination of men.

If liberty is to prevail, the code—the law—and its enforcement, is strictly a social problem and thus is to be left in the hands of a social agency—government. What then is your and my role as unique, independent members of society? It is to think through and to share our best ideas as to government's appropriate role.

One cannot intelligently decide what government should and should not do unless one knows what government is and is not. What is government? I take my cue from Woodrow Wilson: "Government, in the last analysis, is organized

[2]See *Having My Way* (Irvington, N.Y.: The Foundation for Economic Education Inc., 1974), pp. 148-151.

force."[3] In essence, it is a series of edicts backed by a constabulary—a physical force. Obey, or take the consequences!

Let's symbolize this physical force by the clenched fist. Find out what the fist can and cannot do and you will know what government should and should not do, not necessarily what it will and will not do.

What can the fist do? It can inhibit, restrain, prohibit, penalize. What, in all good conscience, should be restrained and penalized? The answer is to be found in the moral codes: fraud, violence, misrepresentations, stealing, predations, killing, that is, all destructive activities.

What can the fist, this physical force, not do? It cannot create. The creative force, in all instances, is a spiritual rather than a physical force, in the sense that discoveries, inventions, insights, intuitive flashes are spiritual. Everything by which we live has its origin in the spiritual before it shows forth in the material. A glass, for instance, is inconceivable had not some cave dweller eons ago discovered how to harness fire. There would be no autos or planes, or any of the countless other material things that grace our lives, had not some Hindu a thousand years ago invented the concept of zero. All modern chemistry, physics, astronomy would be out of the question with only Roman numerals at our disposal. These spiritual forces, since the dawn of consciousness, number in the trillions.

So, how do I draw the line between what government should and should not do? I would have government *limited* to inhibiting and penalizing the destructive actions; leave all creative activities—without exception, education or whatever—

---

[3] *The State* by Woodrow Wilson (Boston: D.C. Heath & Co., 1900), p. 572.

to citizens acting freely, cooperatively, competitively, voluntarily, privately.

Regardless of the miserable historical record of governments overstepping their bounds, limited government is an absolute necessity if liberty is to prevail.

Why is liberty impossible *with* unlimited governments?

Is it liberty if no one is free to act creatively as he pleases? If politicians and bureaucrats are dictating what everyone may and may not produce and exchange, and at what prices? If there be no private ownership—all property owned by government?

It seems clear that unlimited government is tyranny: "Absolute power arbitrarily administered." The administrators of tyranny are tyrants. What is a tyrant? S. C. Champion has brilliantly defined the tyrant as "only the slave turned inside out."

Very well, what is a slave? According to my dictionary, a slave is "a human being who is (1) absolutely subject to another human being" and (2) "a person who is completely dominated by some influence, habit."

In the first sense, then, a tyrant is one absolutely in control of and responsible for another human being. And in the second sense, what is the dominating influence or habit turned inside out? Let's not mince words; it is ignorance parading as infinite wisdom. Such persons proclaim that they can run our lives better than we can.

The folly of tyranny is manifest, whether at the local or national level, or composed of one or 20,000,000 tyrants. All sorts of famous, celebrated, prestigious, small-scale dictators come to mind. So, pick your own from among the highly publicized and then ask yourself how competent he is to run your life. He not only knows nothing about you; he probably doesn't even know you exist. Such tyrants—slaves turned inside out—are notoriously poor at managing their own lives. Why? When one concentrates upon running the lives of others he leaves his own emergence unattended; indeed, one with the slave (tyrant) mentality isn't even aware of his incapacity.

The first step in wisdom is knowing how little one knows, a step that tyrants have not taken. They are slaves transfixed to the driver's seat!

Unlimited government thus places all the people under the domination of slaves. Obviously, liberty is impossible in such a situation.

In the above I have tried to suggest that (1) liberty is impossible short of an understanding of what it is, (2) impossible *without* limited government, and (3) impossible *with* unlimited government.

Now to my contention that everyone loves liberty. Were we to know what it is, aware of the social structure in which it thrives, and willing to pay the price, it is liberty we would have. So, what is liberty?

Liberty is *freedom of choice*. Everyone loves freedom of choice for himself, if not for others; therefore, everyone loves liberty.

Others, of course, may have values or priorities that differ from mine. Their choices are not mine—or vice versa. But does this mean that any of us rejects freedom of choice? Perhaps it will help to list a few among many reasons why I love the freedom to choose:

- To choose my employment, be it a loner in an attic or

working with others, and be it a one-hour day or a hundred-hour week.

- To choose how the fruits of my own labor shall be expended.
- To choose the price at which I am willing to offer my goods and/or services and with whom I shall exchange this or that.
- To choose the books I read or the teachers who may enlighten me.
- To choose my religion.
- To choose the cars I drive, the clothes I wear, the food I eat, that is, what I shall consume.
- To choose when and where I shall travel, be it by foot, on horse, or by plane.
- To choose what I shall think, speak, write, and with whom I may share my thoughts.

If there be anyone who does not favor freedom of choice as much as I do, that person is unknown to me. Thus, my conclusion has to be that everyone loves liberty.

True, a problem arises if and when anyone is unable or unwilling to pay the price or accept the consequences of the choices he makes. Each choice one makes, each action taken, has consequences which impinge upon and affect others, as well as self.

While everyone loves liberty for self, there are ever so many who are unwilling to accord freedom of choice to others. Merely take note of those who favor and endorse wage and price controls, privileges, supports, subsidies, tariffs, quotas, embargoes, the coercive taking from some and giving to others, restrictions on competition; indeed, all deviations from the free market, private ownership, limited government way of life. Note these, and one will have a fair estimate of the number of those who love liberty for self but not for others. They love liberty but *they live license.*[4]

Thus, the love of liberty for self and not for others is but a selfish, greedy, and unattainable dream. Why not be realistic? The formula? The Golden Rule: Do not to others that which you would not have them do unto you. Or, in this context, expect not from others that which you will not happily, graciously, intelligently accord to them! This is how the lovers of liberty may experience what they love. There is no other way. And I, for one, wouldn't have it any other way!

***

A commentary on the chapters that follow:

As Ballvé wrote, "The love of liberty is no less imperishable than the love of knowledge." Hopefully, I have given some support to what appears to be a truism. And, doubtless, Ballvé would reverse his observation and assert that the love of knowledge is no less imperishable than the love of liberty. If true, as it seems to be, then knowledge is as low on the intellectual totem pole as liberty. All will swear that they love knowledge but how few there are who do more than give it lip service!

In any event, the love of liberty and the love of knowledge go hand-in-hand. As people can be free only when self-responsible and self-responsible only when free, so there can be no liberty without knowledge and no knowledge without liberty. These virtues are but two sides of the same intellectual

[4]See "My Freedom Depends On Yours," by Dean Russell. *Essays on Liberty,* Volume II (Irvington, N.Y.: The Foundation for Economic Education, Inc., 1954), pp. 398-420.

and moral coin, descending or ascending in unison. Never expect one without the other!

If you or I would lend a hand to knowledge, and thus to liberty, what should our ambition or determination be? Nothing less than outlined by Thomas Arnold:

> Real knowledge, like everything of value, is not to be attained easily. It must be worked for, studied for, thought for and, more than all, must be prayed for.

The above chapter and those that follow represent no attempt on my part to write a book. Indeed, the above was the last chapter written. What then does this volume represent? Arnold's formula being my own, a thought or an idea now and then comes to mind. Concentrate on each, go wherever honest thinking leads, and share with those who may care for the findings. This is the only contribution I can make to knowledge and thus to liberty.

I make no claim to a single, original idea. No more than some of the phrasing and arrangement of the ideas qualify as original. This is the same theme—in many respects quite repetitive—I have been struggling with for forty years. Why do this? We think in words. Thus, I must try to find those which fit into first this and then that context, my only means for an improved understanding. If at all successful, another may remark, "I *now* see what you mean."

So, gentle reader, please forgive the seeming repetition in this volume—not really a book but, rather, phrasings of several new arrangements put between two covers. This is my umpteenth attempt to give liberty another boost. I love liberty for self—*and others!*

2

LIBERTY: THE GOLDEN MEAN

Socialism is planned chaos; anarchy is unplanned chaos.

Liberty is the golden mean between the two extremes: socialism and anarchy! As to meaning, this bold statement communicates little if anything at first glance, but perhaps there is more than meets the eye. To understand we must dig. Any devotee of liberty likes to be understood, but few of us are. So try and try again!

A mentor of mine had a favorite admonition: "Say what you mean and mean what you say." The latter I may have mastered, but not the former. Saying what one means—communicating what is intended—is world without end. Or should we admit, words without end!

A scholarly book, *The Meaning of Meaning,* dealt with the tyranny of words, the perplexing problem of accurately interpreting another's meaning. On the same theme, Ortega wrote, "Look not in the dictionary for definitions, but to the instant." What did Ortega mean when he said "look . . . to the instant?" My inference is that one should look to the context for clues as to what a writer means by the way he uses words and phrases. The translation from the printed page—or the spoken sentence—to one's mind is a complex affair, and accurate deductions are extremely difficult, often impossible, even if the writer or speaker is saying what he means.

My thesis is that liberty is indeed the golden mean between the two extremes of socialism—*planned chaos*—on the one hand, and anarchy—*unplanned chaos*—on the other. But how many are there who know what I mean by liberty, or socialism, or anarchy? And "golden mean," more often than not, is far from golden. To make sense, the term must be explained as it is here meant. Let me try once more to say what *I* mean when using these words and terms.

According to the dictionary, "golden mean" is defined as "the safe, prudent way between extremes, happy medium; moderation." This can be, and often is, construed to mean a half-way position between any pair of opposites—a mischievous notion. How far from golden would be the "happy medium" between extreme honesty and extreme dishonesty! This would condone dishonesty half the time. In the politico-economic realm we observe "middle-of-the-roaders"—fence straddlers—one leg on the freedom side and the other on the authoritarian side. Such a half-way pose is ridiculous, and far from golden.

To get at my definition of the "golden mean," let me define the two extremes as I mean them.

Socialism is ALL government. It is simply government

ownership and control of the means of production—the planned economy—and the government ownership and control of the results of production—the welfare state.

Why refer to this as planned chaos? Some people insist that this is a contradiction in terms, that nothing could at once be planned and chaotic. Better watch that one! Suppose that I, who know very little about myself, plan the life of you about whom I know nothing and impose my plans by force, leaving you with no freedom of choice—void of free will. Now imagine this same nonsense forcibly imposed on everyone. If such mass enslavement is not chaos, pray tell, what is! And it is "planned"!

Ludwig von Mises in his great book, *Planned Chaos,* devotes chapters to Interventionism, Socialism and Communism, Fascism, Nazism.[1] These, however, along with the Planned Economy and the Welfare State, are but varying labels for the same devilish thing—totalitarianism—*ALL government.* True, each differs in dictatorial gadgetry, but why concern ourselves as to how the firing squad is organized. It is tyrannical by whatever name. To avoid wordiness, call it socialism.

Conceded, regardless of the dictatorial intentions of a Hitler or a Stalin or whoever, the total state has only been approximated, never fully achieved. There is always a leakage of free human energy. Thank God that dictators, foreign and domestic, are not able to carry out their plans all the way. Nonetheless, socialism, by definition and intention, is *ALL government.*

Anarchy is NO government. There are two definitions of

[1] *Planned Chaos* by Ludwig von Mises (Irvington-on-Hudson, N.Y.: The Foundation for Economic Education, Inc., 1965).

this label: (1) "The complete absence of government and law," and (2) "Political disorder and violence." Thus, there are two brands of anarchists: (1) philosophical anarchists who believe only in persuasion and advocate a society with no government and law, and (2) the bomb throwers and activists who personally indulge in violence. My comments on this extreme—the opposite of socialism—are confined to the philosophical anarchists.

One of my favorite thinkers and writers—Leo Tolstoy—was a philosophical anarchist. And I have many friends in today's world who are also of this same persuasion—believers in and advocates of no government or law.

How account for the philosophical anarchists? What prods them to this extreme? In every case known to me, it is a revolt against the idea and practice of socialism. They observe that never has there been a nation but whose government eventually has gone wild, gotten out of bounds, become dictatorial. Their cure for this politico-economic madness? Be rid of government and law—all of it! A parallel tactic would be to remedy the ills of overeating by getting rid of food—all of it!

Why refer to anarchy as "unplanned chaos?" What is a plan? It is "a scheme for making, doing, or arranging something; project, programs; schedule." The anarchists will agree with me that there is nothing whatsoever schematic about their proposed way of life. Its very virtue to them is its unplanned nature. Chaos? It is "any great confusion or disorder." Let me now suggest why anarchy cannot be other than chaotic.

Anarchists, for the most part, do believe in the right of each man to use force in protecting his life, livelihood, property. Their prescription? Let each person buy protection in the market as he buys insurance. Each would, to the extent of his adjudged needs, employ his own bodyguard, gendarme, protector; or perhaps some with kindred interests would band together to buy protection. In short, no social agency—government—and no law applicable to all alike. Instead, there would be individuals, labor unions, corporations, neighborhoods, and countless other entities, each a law unto itself! One can only imagine the resulting chaos, for history reveals no examples of this sort of thing in practice except here and there vigilante committees—utterly chaotic. The practice of anarchy cannot help but be *unplanned chaos,* the opposite extreme of socialism—*planned* chaos. To me, chaos is to be avoided, be it planned or unplanned.

To introduce the concept of liberty—the golden mean—let us assume a society whose citizenry is of unprecedented moral, ethical, intellectual scruples and principles. Not a charlatan in the whole population! Man by nature being imperfect, regardless of how far advanced, there would remain in this imaginary population untold *honest* disagreements: my boundary line is here, not there, as you say; you have misinterpreted our contract; et cetera, et cetera, et cetera.

Is it not evident that law and order are handmaidens? As I see it, there can be no social order in the absence of an adjudicative agency, government, codifying the taboos—law—enforcing an observation thereof, and providing the court of last resort for settling our differences and disagreements.

The truth, so often overlooked, is that each of us is at once an individualistic and social being. This oversight is the seed of much politico-economic nonsense. Yes, let all of us be our individualistic selves, and, by the same token, let government, rather than any you or I, see to it that each of us, while doing our thing, molests no other citizen.[2]

Socialism has never reigned supreme, nor has anarchy. And liberty has only been approximated, more nearly in our country than elsewhere. Indeed, liberty at this moment in history, is rarely even comprehended. What then is liberty?

Liberty is that situation in which government is limited to inhibiting all destructive actions—foreign and domestic—in a word, keeping the peace; and the law limited to invoking a common justice—to one and all the same! No control over any peaceful, creative activity! Liberty includes that state of affairs where the blindfolded goddess of justice does not peek, as today, and say, "Tell me who you are and I shall tell you what your rights are."

With the formal societal agency thus limited, every citizen is free to act creatively as he pleases. This is the free and unfettered market with the creative actions of the millions flowing without let or hindrance to each in proportion to his own creative and productive contributions. Law and order, government and the free market in a working and harmonious relationship!

Liberty, as defined in its ideal form, is truly the *golden* mean between the extremes of socialism and anarchy. Attainable? I suspect not, for man is imperfect. Can it be more nearly approximated than ever before in history? Indeed, it can! Merely keep the golden mean in our minds and exercise eternal vigilance—stand now and forever against any and all deviations from Liberty: Freedom of choice—The Ideal!

---

[2]For an explanation of the necessity for government and its appropriate role, see *Government: An Ideal Concept* (Irvington-on-Hudson, N.Y.: The Foundation for Economic Education, Inc., 1954), pp. 5-49.

3
FINDING WORDS FOR COMMON SENSE

No man has a prosperity so high or firm, but that two or three words can dishearten it; and there is no calamity which right words will not begin to redress.

—**EMERSON**

For years I have contended that no one—past or present—has more than scratched the surface when it comes to making the case for the free society. Friends of freedom exhibit two shortcomings: (1) a scanty understanding of why freedom works its miracles, and (2) an inability to explain clearly enough such understanding as we presently possess.

For the sake of this thesis, assume some knowledge of why authoritarianism is doomed to failure and why only freedom makes creativity possible; man needs freedom if he is to grow in awareness, perception, consciousness, that is to say, achieve his earthly purpose. To embrace the free as opposed to the authoritarian way of life is just common sense: "practical judgment or intelligence; ordinary good sense." The problem? Finding common words to clearly explain what we mean.

Not until writing "The Police: Friend or Foe?" (see chapter 16) had it ever occurred to me that hardly anyone knows what we mean by our commonly used term "limited government." Why? The term is too abstract; no one has ever seen a government!

So, use "police" instead. Everyone has seen police. That's a word for common sense. This, however, only opens the eye to the problem, and we need to bring the full range of our powers to bear, for the problem is endless and confronts us in every thought we express. The tyranny of words! But, as Emerson promises, "there is no calamity which right words will not *begin* to redress." I do not pretend to know many of the right words, but I think I know a few wrong ones—words that do not now make common sense.

Let's begin with what was once a perfectly excellent and fairly understood term: *laissez faire. Laissez* means to *let* and *faire* means *to do.* This was the maxim of the French free-trade economists of the 18th century, suggesting that government should not interfere in peaceful industrial affairs and uncoerced trade; in a word, freedom to produce, to exchange, to travel. Ludwig von Mises concludes an enlightening and excellent chapter with these words: *"Laissez faire* means: let the individual citizen, the much talked-about common man, choose and act and do not force him to yield to a dictator."[1]

---

[1]See Chapter III—"Laissez Faire Or Dictatorship" in *Planning for Freedom* by Ludwig von Mises (Libertarian Press, South Holland, Illinois).

The question is, should we devotees of the free market—who would limit the police to a defensive role and to invoking a common justice—use *laissez faire* to label our politico-economic position? My answer is No! and for good reason: the opponents of freedom have so effectively defamed and smeared the term that nearly all untutored readers or listeners will think of us as greedy blackguards. John Maynard Keynes in his *The End of Laissez Faire* (1926) and an Oxford Professor and author of detective stories—G. D. H. Cole—writing in the *Encyclopaedia of the Social Sciences* (1933) lent their name and fame to the verbal muckraking that had been going on for many decades. They have succeded in rendering a good term useless.

Imagine!—advancing their opposition to freedom not by reason and logic, not by appeals to common sense—but by twisting words and meanings.

So, it is up to us to find words that lend themselves less to verbal chicanery, words that are not so vulnerable, words that make it possible for others to glean what we really mean. In this instance, what might it be? How about using a phrase that implies the same virtues as *laissez faire:* "A fair field and no favor?" Let them try to advance their socialism by advocating an unfair field and special favors to some at the expense of others! A fair field, with no favor is a phrasing which nicely summarizes our position and has the added merit of putting the antagonists of freedom on the defensive.

Labels, it seems to me, have turned out to be booby traps. Merely observe how our very own labels have been turned against us, even such a great word as Liberalism. To the classical economist and other heirs of the Whig tradition, Liberalism meant a freeing of the individual from the tyranny of an omnipotent police. Observe what liberalism now means: police liberality with the fruits of your and my livelihood! Should we then not resort to labels? Ideas need some sort of designation, so why not find words to better explain our ideas and ideals?

Reflect on another label, Capitalism. Many of the best free market thinkers known to me label our way of life "capitalism." In my view this loaded word conjures up as many different notions of what we mean as there are persons who hear and read that label. Small wonder, for the term was given currency by Karl Marx as a means of smearing the freedom philosophy! It came into the vocabulary as a dirty word; turning it into a pretty word to aid and abet common sense may well be beyond our skills.

What about Democracy as a label for the free society? I would never use the word to describe our ideal. Why not? Simply because—like the word Capitalism—it utterly fails to communicate meaning accurately. Definitions of Democracy range all the way from Abraham Lincoln's "the government of the people, by the people, for the people" to James Russell Lowell's "the bludgeoning of the people, by the people, for the people." To millions of citizens, Democracy means no more than a system of deciding basic politico-economic principles by counting noses, that is, by majority vote.

What to do? My suggestion: find words to spell out, explain, define what we mean, as did Edmund Opitz in his "The American System and Majority Rule."[2] "The Police: Friend or Foe?" was an attempt on my part at finding words for common sense. Neither one of us had done more in these pieces

---

[2]See "The American System and Majority Rule," *The Freeman*, November 1962. Reprint available on request.

than try to discover phrasings and explanations to replace noncommunicative labeling. These are but beginnings on our part at what seem to be correct method—nothing more. Required, if there is to be a better understanding and practice of liberty, is that hundreds or thousands go to work to make common sense of the main idea—find the right words.

I am now convinced that finding words for common sense must be the *first* step in gaining an understanding of why the free market—with the police limited to invoking a common justice and keeping the peace—works its miracles. Until now, I have had it the other way around! I have been urging that, first, we must understand why the free market has a wisdom unimaginably greater than exists in any discrete individual, and only second, find the words to explain the miracle. I was wrong—finding the right words comes first! Without them there's no explaining the miracle.

All of us do our thinking in words. Words are the means; and, if they be right, revelation or enlightenment is the end—the product thereof. Today's calamity—the police power omnipotent—is disheartening. But, "there is no calamity which right words will not begin to redress."

If we find the words to limit the police establishment to its proper role, a light will shine forth: an understanding of why the free market works its miracles.

4

THE MATERIAL: A SOURCE OF LIFE

Everything is first worked out in the unseen before it is manifested in the seen, in the ideal before it is realized in the real, in the spiritual before it shows forth in the material.

—RALPH WALDO TRINE

Far be it from me to explain the coming of life onto this earth. So, my theme is not *the* source, but, rather, *a* source of life. The material—a sufficiency of goods and services—has a far more important role in our lives than is generally realized. Merely observe how often material abundance is denigrated, as if it were an evil instead of a blessing.

Reflect on the population in the land that is now the U.S.A., say, 400 years ago—primitive America. While there was no official census at that time, it is estimated that the Indian population numbered fewer than 1,000,000. Why such a small number of people in this vast continent? It wasn't because of a lack of natural resources; there were more then than now. Nor was it because those people were unable to bear offspring.

There was one reason and one only: a foraging economy could feed only a small number of people, and even these few lived in what we would call abject poverty.

Today, the population in this once underdeveloped country is around 220,000,000. The reason for our enlarged population? Material progress and development! The obvious deduction? Were it not for the material improvement, the chances are 220 to one that you and I would not have been born; we would not have experienced life. Thus, these things material are indeed *a* source of life.

All history tells of the rise and then the decline and fall of nations. Look around at today's world. Will the U.S.A. prove an exception to the rule? My answer: Only if some of us come to a far better understanding than now of the relationship between material progress and human life. 'Tis a learning problem, and we'll learn or perish! At least we have a choice.

Ralph Waldo Trine suggests some thoughts which, if fully grasped, may help in our learning.

The unseen and the seen. Well over a century ago, Frederic Bastiat wrote a brilliant essay, "What is Seen and What is Not Seen."[1] One of his illustrations: A lad broke a windowpane. All the onlookers thought this a beneficial act, for what would become of the glaziers if no one ever broke a window! *This is what is seen.*

However, *it is not seen* that the six francs paid for a new windowpane would have been spent to replace a worn-out pair of shoes or a new book for the library. The shoe industry (or some other) would have received six francs' worth of encouragement.

[1]*Selected Essays On Political Economy* (Irvington-on-Hudson, N.Y.: The Foundation for Economic Education, Inc., 1968).

Anyone who can think beyond the *seen* to the *unseen* takes a big step toward becoming a good economist.

Inspired by Bastiat's way of seeing into the nature of economic behavior, I once wrote a short article featuring two photographs, one of a governmentally owned power and light plant, the other of a privately owned power and light plant.[2] In the photos—to the eye, the seen—the two plants appear identical. But the unseen back of each one? As different as black and white!

The unseen is perceived by the mind, if at all, and it is this perception that reveals differences between the two plants:

	Government Plant	**Private Plant**
Capital:	Expropriated	Voluntarily invested
Management:	Politically chosen	Based on performance
Labor:	Civil servants	Openly competitive
Accounting:	Political guesswork	Profit and loss
Result:	Barren socialism	Creative freedom

The ideal and the real. At the time of primitive America, there popped into the head of Leonardo da Vinci an ideal: man flying through the air as do birds. While the contraption he designed on paper wouldn't fly, several centuries later his ideal became real. Assuredly the idea must precede the finished product.

In World War I airplane pilots had no parachutes. However, there were many who had the ideal in mind: being able to jump from a plane and land in safety. Many a pilot was saved during World War II because the idea had become the reality of a parachute.

---

[2] *The Freeman,* October 1957.

Peace between and after these wars witnessed another ideal: flying so safely that there was no need for parachutes. The real? Based on passenger-miles, flying today is far safer than driving.

The above is only to illustrate Trine's truth: "Everything is worked out . . . in the ideal before it is realized in the real."

The spiritual and the material. Professor Ludwig von Mises saw eye-to-eye with Trine on this point:

> Production [the material] is a spiritual, intellectual, and ideological phenomenon. It is the method that man, directed by reason, employs for the best possible removal of uneasiness. What distinguishes our conditions from those of our ancestors who lived one thousand or twenty thousand years ago is not something material but something spiritual. The material changes are the outcome of spiritual changes.[3]

Though most of us in America today owe our very lives to these material achievements, we take them for granted. And rarely do we appreciate that every material gain stems *exclusively* from a spiritual origin—intellectual accomplishments of the mind. Thus, we owe our lives to ideas unimaginable to the Indians of 400 years ago.

Think of it! Telephones rather than smoke signals! The human voice around the earth in the same fraction of a second a warwhoop could be heard fifty yards away! Countless millions of goods and services Indians never dreamed of and most of which we in our day have never heard of! For example, of several hundred thousand companies in the U.S.A., one alone makes over 200,000 items and not a man in the

[3]*Human Action* (Chicago: Henry Regnery Company. Third Revised Edition, 1966) p. 142.

company knows precisely what they are. And all because of a remarkable spiritual growth!

What is meant by spiritual in this context? It is the unseen and the ideal which precedes the seen and the real—spiritual in the sense that reason, ideas, insights, intuitive flashes, inventions, discoveries are spiritual. It is the inspired and higher outcroppings of the mind that spawn—give birth to—extensions of the material, to the multiplication of life. Hail to the spiritual!

Crawford Greenewalt perceived clearly what I am trying to explain about the spiritual: "Behind every advance of the human race is a germ of creation growing in the mind of some lone individual—an individual whose dreams awaken him in the night while others lie contentedly asleep."

Back to the Indians of long ago, they knew how to set wood afire; and it was flaming wood alone that they used for heat, light and cookery. I shall not attempt here to describe the advances in heating and cookery, but let me cite examples in the field of lighting. When I was a small lad a remarkable kerosene lamp had come into existence. Why remarkable? Not a person, even to this day, knows all the intricate steps required to produce kerosene or to make the globe of a lamp—no more than any individual knows how to make a pencil. What then? A "germ of creation"—the spiritual—growing in the minds of countless lone individuals and configurating. A new light—the miracle of the market!

Later, came the Coleman lamp, giving ever so much more light than the original kerosene lamp. And still later, the electric bulb. No one knows what electricity is. However, a combination of reasons, ideas, insights, intuitive flashes, inventions, discoveries—spiritual forces—have harnessed this mysterious radiant force so that we now use it not only for lighting but for heating and cooking. The spiritual shows forth in the material—*a* source of life!

Will the U.S.A. prove an exception to the rule? Or will we suffer the usual historical pattern of a decline and fall? The answer lies in learning what we should discourage on the one hand and encourage on the other.

What discourage? Authoritarianism however labeled: socialism, communism, the welfare state, the planned economy, political dictocrats running our lives. Whenever authoritarianism prevails, when most of us are but carbon copies of shortsighted rulers, we face *a return to primitivism!* In brief, we are destined for a decline and fall with the eventual disappearance of the material sources of life! The role of government is to protect rather than to run our lives. Summarized, those who like to dominate are evidencing a primitive trait as are those who prefer to be dominated. This trait, if recognized and understood, should be discouraged.

What to encourage? It is more or less plain that "germs of creation" can spawn only in the minds of men who are free to act creatively as they choose. And this means everyone; for, as the creative record attests, the ones from whom the spiritual emerges are never known beforehand, by themselves, or by anyone else. Whoever foresaw a Marconi or an Edison!

Far less plain is the necessity of freedom for a configuration of the "germs of creation." In the absence of freedom they cannot configurate or materialize and, thus, die aborning. All material items—a pencil, a light bulb, a jet plane, or whatever—are the results, the finished manifestation, the combining or materializing of literally millions or trillions of infinitesimal thoughts and antecedent "germs" going back to the harnessing of fire. Freedom is the key to all of these material things by which we live and prosper.

Finally, why are so many people led into "thinking" otherwise? I suspect it is because of a wrong correlation. People observe authoritarianism gaining by leaps and bounds, with material abundance far greater than in any other nation. The dictocrats claim the credit, and too many citizens believe them.

The truth? The abundance we still enjoy is exclusively the result of a leakage of free human energy. Our present blessings are in spite, not because, of political domineering. Dictocrats and their ways are the seen; freedom is the unseen. Again, anyone who can think beyond the *seen* to the *unseen* takes a long step toward becoming a good economist and toward assuring the material, *a* source of life. May their tribe increase!

5

LEARN HOW TO LIVE WITH WEALTH!

We don't know what's happening to us, and that's precisely what's happening to us.

—**ORTEGA**

Most people today feel in their bones that something is askew. They may not know what it is or how to find out. Ortega was right, we don't know what's happening to us. If we knew—

One thing is certain: Material prosperity is ours, and we must learn how to live with wealth—as the owner of property—or face the alternative of learning how to survive in poverty. For the former, there is a prescription; for the latter, I am unaware of one that satisfies.

Let's reflect for a moment on some common misconceptions about learning or, rather, the lack of conceptions. For isn't it true that persons, with rare exceptions, are quite complacent in this respect? Pleased at whatever level they find themselves? Little awareness of knowing next to nothing and, thus, no driving urge to learn and learn and learn, now and always!

Actually, "graduation"—I have arrived—seems to be the common stagnating mood rather than "commencement"—I am beginning—the emerging aspiration. This explains, as much as anything, why we don't know what's happening to us.

What's new? Everything in everyone's life and at all times! One must *learn* to live as best he can in whatever situation he finds himself, no two moments being the same: friendly and unfriendly associations, locations in this or that part of the world, booms and busts, charlatans and/or statesmen in office, ups and downs of all kinds—including poverty *and* wealth.

Wealth? Never in the world's history have any people been so abundantly graced with goods and services as are present-day Americans. Indeed, the material items available for purchase are so numerous that no one of us has even heard of many of those things. Among us are thousands of millionaires who, only seven generations ago, would have been serfs. Then reflect on the mill run of us—the you's and me's—who engage in minor specializations in exchange for which we obtain countless material things my grandfather could not have imagined, let alone possessed. Further, think of the people who "never turn a finger," yet live in unprecedented luxury. No ancient lord of the manor remotely approached the material status of most Americans of our day.

Please bear in mind that I am using the term, wealth, in its popular sense: dollar value, property, purchasing power. But let me not leave the impression that increasing wealth is life's supreme purpose. That's not my thesis. However, even in that sense of the word, the question, "who's wealthy?" evokes other questions, "compared to whom?" and "in whose judgment?" It all depends upon one's sense of values as to whether he deems himself rich or poor. Value judgments! A starving man may value an apple more than a millionaire would value another thousand dollars. In any event, *all* Americans, in a strict material sense, are wealthy "beyond belief" compared to people in Calcutta; indeed, to most of the world's population.

In light of the above, what then is my thesis? *Not only must "poor" people learn to live with others wealthier than they are but, equally important, "rich" people must learn to live with their own wealth!* With rare exceptions, this kind of learning is neither attempted nor achieved. Learn to live with wealth, regardless of material status, or expect its disappearance from the face of the earth. That's my thesis!

As a starter, we must gain an awareness of the cause of America's unprecedented wealth. During the nineteenth century, governors of other nations, amazed that such a fantastic thing could happen so quickly in what had been a really underdeveloped country, sent commissions to find the answer. After all, their nations were old, they had "experienced leaders," and their lands too were graced with fertile soils, friendly climates, natural resources. What could the answer be!

So far as the record shows, not a single commission got the point. Tocqueville, who made a deep study of the American phenomenon, discovered or uncovered the fundamental reason:

> I sought for the greatness and genius of America in fertile fields and boundless forests; it was not there. I sought for it in her free schools and her institutions of learning; it was not there. I sought for it in her matchless Constitution and

democratic congress; it was not there. Not until I went to the churches of America and found them aflame with righteousness did I understand the greatness and genius of America. America is great because America is good. When America ceases to be good, America will cease to be great.

True! Without the goodness to which Tocqueville refers, there would have been no miracle. Nor would there have been that "matchless Constitution" and the Bill of Rights. These were secondary but vitally important because they limited organized force—government—more severely than ever before in all history. In a word, there was very little standing against the release of creative energy. A veritable outburst of creativity! Why? If the reason isn't obvious, it should be.

But first, why must the rich learn to live with their wealth? Unless they do they will, as in most cases, become do-nothings, know-nothings, joining the growing ranks of those who demand protection in their idleness. Learning to live with wealth is elementary as the ABC's. Wealth is no warrant to get out of life, to vegetate, to become work-less and worthless. On the contrary, its purpose is to get us ever deeper into life, to free the individual from the slavery which abject poverty imposes. It is the means by which one may discover his own uniqueness and work harder than ever at its realization and perfection. Property is the extension of man, a part of the talents with which he is endowed and for the development of which he is responsible.

Wealth, viewed in its proper sense, is a means of increasing one's own creativity, a phase in the evolution of the human race. Are there such exemplary persons? Yes, I am acquainted with several multi-millionarires who think only of their work and nothing at all of their enormous wealth. They are learned men and their capital is productively invested—to the boon of mankind.

Being born wealthy is much like being born with any other special gift or talent. That talent may be used constructively to serve self and others; or it may be abused to harm others and destroy oneself.

While I will concede no advantage to being born poor, it is wonderful to be born in a country where intelligent hard work will bring its reward—as *has been* true of the America we have known. Reflect on the reverse: living in a country with no wealth—all poor. Hard work would be meaningless. So, let the poor learn to live with wealth, their opportunity to grow. Short of this, they will crumble further the foundations that accounted for the America we have known. How explain the outburst of creativity which, if not obvious, should be?

Tocqueville clearly and, in my opinion, correctly identified the fundamental reason: a people "aflame with righteousness." His was but an affirmation of an ancient enlightenment: "Seek ye first the Kingdom of God [Truth and Righteousness], and these things [wealth, learning, intelligence] shall be added unto you." C. S. Lewis phrased it thus, "Aim at Heaven and you get earth thrown in. Aim at earth and you will get neither."

Given righteousness as the foundation, there followed as an outgrowth an unprecedented limitation of governmental action. For the first time in history there was little if anything standing against the freeing, releasing of creative human energy. Thus, the outburst, the American miracle—freedom on a scale never before experienced in the world's history!

Reflect again on the commissions sent by the governors of

other nations to find the reason for the American miracle. Had they succeeded, their report would have read as follows:

1. Our own case is hopeless short of a free and self-responsible people;
2. Further, we must have a citizenry aflame with righteousness, and bent on thinking for self and learning that governments never bestow any wealth on anyone except as it is taken from someone else.
3. If such a phenomenal improvement in thinking can be assumed, our governor must substantially dismantle his dictocratic establishment.

But not one of the commissions got the point!

The commissions did not get the point, nor do most present-day Americans. It is this and this alone: *All wealth has its origin in the context of freedom—no man-concocted restraints against the release of creative human energy.* Not an iota of wealth results from governments taking from some and giving to others. If this isn't obvious, it ought to be!

As things now stand in our country, the idle rich, not knowing why, side with socialistic remedies to bring about the New Jerusalem. And the relatively poor—few are really poor—are blinded to their opportunities by envy and fall into the same authoritarian trap. Thus, the mess we're in!

The remedy as I see it? Work and learn! If what one does to make a living isn't joyous, what, then, can be the point of living? And learn to live with wealth, that is, come to an understanding of its origin and an appreciation of its blessings and evolutionary purpose. Talents and wealth used joyfully point the way to a better life—a life improved through service, not only to self, but to mankind.

6

THOSE THINGS CALLED MONEY

What this country needs is a good five-cent nickel.

—ED WYNN

Nearly everyone at this moment of money madness will agree with Wynn's statement—humorous but sound. H. B. Bohn remarked: "Of money, wit, and virtue, believe one-fourth of what you hear." As to wit and virtue, Bohn may be right. But I doubt that as much as a fourth of what we hear about money is worth serious consideration, for most of the pronouncements stem from a premise that it is a function of government to issue money and regulate the value thereof. The premise seems wrong to me. I believe that if money is to be useful to traders as a medium of exchange then the decisions as to what shall serve as money must be worked out by traders in the market, *voluntarily,* rather than by governmental edict.

If you are further interested in what I believe, reflect for a moment on the various commodities and other things that have been used for money: wampum, sea shells, salt, fur, dried fish, ivory, cigarettes, silk stockings, gold and other metals—the list is long. These are some of the things called money, but note that of those listed thus far, all are commodities that, at the time, were in common use in trade—so common that they were useful as a medium of exchange.

But things of a different category, "non-commodities," also are called money—and thereby hangs our tale. German marks are things; in 1923 five billion of these things wouldn't buy a loaf of bread. Paper dollars also are things called money—legal tender—government money which the law requires a creditor to accept in payment of a debt. Or to put it another way, government money, if created out of thin air by edict, is in no sense a scarce and valuable resource useful to traders but is rather a means of taxing or taking scarce resources from the market without offering anything useful in exchange. Such "money" may be a clever form of taxation, but it is far worse than useless as a medium of exchange.

Am I arguing that government money never has been "worth a Continental?" Not necessarily. If a government issues paper receipts that are fully backed by some valuable and widely acceptable item of trade—fully redeemable upon demand by the bearer—such receipts may serve very well as a medium of exchange. But, of course, there's no reason on earth why the issuance of warehouse receipts should be a governmental function. Let anyone do it who has a warehouse, and printing press, and a sufficient stock of gold or silver or whatever else the receipt calls for. And let government intervene only to see that the receipts are not fraudulent—counterfeit.

I am well aware that some governments of some nations at some times have been in charge of monetary policy with quite satisfactory results, when the policy was to mint standardized coins and issue receipts fully redeemable in some well-known and highly marketable commodity. But there is no reason to suppose that the managers of a governmental monopoly will long function in competitive fashion if the monopoly can be exploited to gain additional political power. And it doesn't take a genius to figure how to exploit a money monopoly: just print bogus warehouse receipts and declare them to be legal tender; then pass laws to penalize suppliers of goods or services who refuse to accept the bogus receipts at face value. Finally, this can be pushed to the point of issuing receipts based not on the *fullness* of the warehouse but on its *emptiness* instead—the use of the national debt as the backing for the paper money.

What would be the grossest fraud if an individual tried it has become the common practice of governments—all quite legal because it is a governmental monopoly. And the result is a runaway inflation that disrupts business activities and hinders rather than facilitates trade. This is why governments cannot be trusted with power to determine what traders should use as a medium of exchange. Let the traders choose. Leave the decisions about money to the market. Limit the government to its proper function of policing the market and punishing traders who cheat or rob or willfully injure other peaceful persons.

When I say that decisions about money should be left to the market, I do not presume to know precisely what those decisions might be. Nor do I find much agreement among monetary experts as to what those decisions ought to be. Would traders insist on pure gold as money? Would they use checking accounts or American Express or credit cards? Would they patronize banks and insist on 100 per cent reserves? I don't know, and I'm not terribly concerned that no one else seems to know precisely. What I am concerned about is that men be free to choose whatever best seems to serve their own respective purposes. And I believe that from such freedom to succeed or fail in open competition in the market will come the most nearly perfect and tamper-proof monetary policy humanly possible.

How much understanding of money is required of us? No more understanding than any one of us has about how to make a jet airplane.

To support this point, let me repeat for the umpteenth time that no single person knows how to make an ordinary wooden lead pencil, explained in a brevity entitled, "I, Pencil."[1] Yet, the year that piece was written, we made in the U.S.A. 1,600,000,000 wooden pencils. How come? How explain a knowhow that exists in no one of us, even remotely? My answer: It is the overall luminosity, the wisdom in the free market. When millions of people are free to act creatively as they choose, an unimaginable wisdom is the consequence. To assert that it is a billion times greater than exists in any discrete individual would be a gross understatement.

Keep in mind that any single person's understanding of how money could be made to serve us honestly and efficiently is precisely as impossible as understanding how to make a pencil!

It is appropriate at this point to ask a question to which no one has a correct answer: What would be the medium-of-exchange situation were it left not to dictocratic control but to the fantastic wisdom of the market? To hazard a guess would be to feign a clairvoyance beyond human experience.

---

[1]See "I, Pencil," *The Freeman,* December 1958.

Guessing would be as farfetched as expecting Socrates to have foreseen and described the makings of present-day air travel, electric lighting, the human voice delivered around the earth in one-seventh of a second, my dictaphone, or a thousand and one other phenomena. I call these "phenomena" because no one understands or can describe the genesis of these countless economic blessings even after their existence! The wisdom that accounts for them is not in you or me; it derives from the overall lunimosity. *Why then should we not entrust money—the medium of exchange—to this same wisdom rather than to the coercive power of those now in public office?*

Yes, what this country needs is a good five-cent nickel. The way is clear: Relegate organized force—government—to the defense of life and property, invoking a common justice, keeping the peace. And leave all creative activities, including the medium of exchange—money—to the wisdom of the market. Do this or our country will end up with a five-cent thousand-dollar bill.

Difficult? Yes! Impossible? Who knows! One thing for certain: Turning money affairs over to the free market is no more an idealistic dream than reducing government to its proper role. And, another thing for certain: Standing for that which seems politically expedient or feasible gains nothing; such techniques are doomed to failure. On the other hand, every boon to mankind has had its birth in the pursuit and upholding of what's right. Humanity has been graced with many boons, every one of which was first thought to be impossible. Bear in mind that righteousness, as well as faith, works miracles.

7

THE COSTWORD PUZZLE

It is easy to be generous with other people's money.

—JOHN RAY

There was a time, many years ago, when I enjoyed crossword puzzles. Today I am more interested in ways to explain what might be called the "costword" puzzle. Understanding basic liberty no longer remains my problem—or so I believe—but discovering how to explain the price, value, and cost phase of the philosophy simply enough that another might understand—this is the challenge! As yet, I haven't scratched the surface. *Simple* explanation remains the challenge! Frankly, few if any puzzles in the politico-economic realm have had less unravelling than this one, and it may be that none is more important to master.

Why the confusion, the difficulty? Why so near an insoluble puzzle? The dilemma: it is a truism that prices, values, and costs as related to the free market are understood by only a few; and the same may be said for prices, values, and costs as related to government. When neither one is understood, *no distinction is made between them.* The fact? They are as different as light and dark, not only in their meaning but in their effect. A costword puzzle, indeed!

First, let us reflect on free market prices. They are determined by supply and demand, that is, by entrepreneurial ingenuity and consumer acceptance. While the buyer has the final say-so, it is the seller—producer—who uses scarce resources in ways that more efficiently serve consumers and is thus responsible for all of us getting more for less.

To illustrate, go back to Henry Ford's horseless carriage. The buyers were close to nil. So how come there are perhaps 100,000,000 cars on the roads today? Entrepreneurial excellence and buyer's assent! While the consumer is king, the producer is kingpin!

One more example: Suppose there is no more demand for my services as a lecturer than there was in the beginning for Ford's horseless carriage, regardless of how low my offer. The price? Zero! What can be done? I can try to improve, as some others have done until they now receive $5,000 per lecture—the price at which the supply of such quality lectures and the demand for them fall into equilibrium. I can try to improve my competence, but the buyer decides what the lecture is worth.

Why is it so important that you and I grasp the scissorlike manner in which free market prices are set? Unless we do, we'll fall into the popular fallacy supported by most politicians, labor union officials, a vast majority of classroom "economists," and even by many businessmen. Their one-sided stand? Sellers set the prices; consumers are but their pawns!

Observe this mischievous notion in action. Remember several years ago when newspapers across the nation displayed pictures of women toting placards, parading in front of stores as pickets are wont to do, demanding lower prices.

They thought the owners—sellers—were solely responsible for the high prices.

Less than 200 years ago:

> The washerwomen of Paris, finding soap so dear that they could hardly purchase it, insisted that all the merchants should be punished by death. . . . Marat [Member, National Assembly] declared loudly that the people, by hanging shopkeepers and plundering stores, could easily remove the trouble.[1]

Marat's solution, applying his own formula had he been a sound economist, would have been suicide! Why? He and his economically illiterate tribe were the source of the trouble. But more on that later.

Second, what about free market value determination? What is the value of this or that good or service? The idea is simple enough, though general confusion may well originate with the economists' terminology: "the subjective theory of value."

How simplify? Subjective means that I determine the value of things to me—perhaps not a precise number or price for anything but close enough to arrange that thing in my personal scale of values, higher than some alternatives, lower than others. Each individual establishes his own scale of values in the light of conditions as he sees them at any moment in time. Conditions may change, and so does the arrangement of any individual's subjective scale of values.

If I am hungry, I may place a higher value on a bowl of soup than on an overcoat, might even value a second or third

---

[1]Andrew Dickson White, *Fiat Money Inflation in France* (Irvington, N.Y.: The Foundation for Economic Education, 1959) pp. 71-72.

bowl of soup above an overcoat. Under other conditions, I might value an overcoat above an automobile. One need only reflect on his own shifting, varying, ever-changing judgments of value as manifested in the exchanges he makes, the buying or selling he does day in and day out. That's all there is to the subjective theory of value—the free market way whereby I assess the value of goods and services to me.

Third, what about costs in a free market, private ownership, *limited government* way of life where competition—domestic and foreign—prevails and there are no man-concocted restraints against the release of creative human energy? The results are so phenomenal that they stagger the imagination!

While the ideal has never existed, it was approximated in the U.S.A. more than elsewhere, at least enough to demonstrate that costs—and prices—have had, *until recently,* a fantastic record of dropping from an original high to lower and lower levels. Recall the original ball point pen? $14.00! Later, competitors found ways to reduce costs—and prices—to the point that several dozen better pens could be purchased for that amount. This is but one among countless millions of examples.

One more: what would it have cost my great-grandfather to go from New York to San Francisco? Months of labor and hardship, perhaps his life. So remarkable has the free market worked its wonders in innovation and cost reduction that his modern counterpart could go from coast to coast and back again in less time than my great-grandfather labored each day and at the cost of a very few days of labor at present wages.

An entrepreneur, the head of a large oil company, discovered ways to refine oil at lower cost than his competitors. By the time they had caught up with him, his company had made hundreds of millions. And by that time he had found more ways to cut costs. In the free market, profits are realized not by above-market pricing but by cutting costs. Who benefits? True, the most successful producers are enriched. However, others like to make money too and are inspired to try their hand. Though many fail, the record shows that some of those who try leapfrog the ones out front. The real beneficiaries? The masses, the millions of consumers—the you's and I's. In the free market, the successful producers, the ones out front, regardless of how much they make, are our servants. Hail to the cost cutters!

Entrepreneurs make headway only as they find ways to reduce costs. However, there is a cost which they do not control: the price tag that goes with an ever-expanding, runaway government. Cut costs in countless ways as they are inspired to do and there comes crashing down upon them the enormous costs of government, federal, state, and local—financed in large measure by inflation.

Inflation is governmental dilution of the money supply as a means to syphon private property into the coffers of government. As a consequence, government's paper money is worth less and less, putting more and more producers out of business and resulting in less and less purchasing power on the part of consumers. Entrepreneurs, as producers, have no more control over this political legerdemain than they have over the thoughts of a Karl Marx or another's passion for power. This explains why, as a result of inflation and regardless of entrepreneurial ingenuity, prices nowadays keep going up and up rather than down and down.

Next, reflect on the distinction between free market and governmental value. Instead of the subjective theory of value—I determine the value of things to me—it is the *arbitrary* theory of value—the dictocrats determine the value of things to me.

But arbitrary and subjective aren't quite adequate to explain the marked distinctions here at issue. Much of what government does—TVA, the Gateway Arch, government schools, public housing, the postal system, et cetera, et cetera, et cetera—presumably is justified according to the labor theory of value, a Marxian theorem. Value is supposedly derived from the cost of production, that is, the amount and cost of labor required determines value. Absurd? Yes, when simplified: Were the same amount of labor employed to make a mud pie as an apple pie, the two pies would have an equal value! Consumers, however, when free to choose, will exchange more—ever so much more—for apple pies than for mud pies. But when values are determined by government, they have no choice. This explains why so much of our property is taken for the production of governmental mud pies.

And last, what about the distinction between free market and governmental prices? As far apart as up and down! When the market is free, the consumers wear the badge of authority.[2] When government is in the politico-economic driver's seat, politicans, bureaucrats, and their coercive allies, labor unions, sport that badge. They set our prices. How? By wage and price controls, rationing, embargoes, quotas, tariffs, below market hours and above market wages, what and

[2]"Caveat Emptor: The Consumer's Badge of Authority," by Bertel M. Sparks, *The Freeman,* June 1975.

how much and with whom we may exchange, what we may sow and grow and the quantities thereof. Food prices? Zero for the 16,000,000 recipients of food stamps, and higher and higher prices for the rest of us. Insurance? Zero for those who receive unemployment insurance. Doctors? By reason of government's interventions into the practice of medicine, the rates are now so high that many doctors are quitting their practice. Delivery? The free market delivers four pounds of oil from the Persian Gulf to our eastern seaboard for less money than government delivers a 2-ounce letter across the street in one's home town! To list similar distinctions in their entirety would require a very long book.

Why these fantastic distinctions? Free market pricing goes down and down by reason of innovations and cost-cutting. Consumers are the beneficiaries. Government pricing goes down only in those instances where the earnings of some are coercively taken and given to others for nothing or next to nothing. Consumers who are not recipients of this legal plunder are victims rather than beneficiaries. Merely note how the cost of government goes up and up whenever and to the extent that governmental prices are arbitrarily lowered. Talk about political legerdemain! And all because there are so few if any who are able to explain simply enough the utter fallacy of authoritarianism.

Perhaps John Ray put his finger on the political trickery that beleaguers most of us: "It is easy to be generous with other people's money." Generosity I favor but with my property, not yours!

The challenge? Let each of us try better to work or decipher this costword puzzle. The reward? A civilized rather than a barbaric society!

8
THE ROOTS OF CONCORD AND DISCORD

If a house be divided against itself,
that house cannot stand.

—**MARK III: 25**

The house we call America is divided against itself, as is evident to anyone who has eyes to see and ears to hear. Discord is rampant; concord is rare. This is a social matter: citizens at ugly odds with each other—discord—or, on the other hand, citizens in more or less harmonious relationships—concord. If our house is to stand, concord must replace discord and, if this is to be accomplished, we must practice the way of life that leads to harmony.

What road are we now treading? It's the road to serfdom. Day by day and in nearly every way, we move nearer to omnipotent government, the totalitarian state—dictocrats by the millions telling us how to live our lives. I believe there is an infallible guideline as to whether the wrong or right road is being trod. It is this: *When discord is rampant, we're on the wrong road; when concord prevails, we're on the right one.*

What is the road in the opposite direction? It is the free market, private ownership, limited government way of life. Not a single dictocrat—those in government confined to invoking a common justice and keeping the peace. In a word, no man-concocted restraints standing against the release of creative human energy.

Now to the big questions. Why does the road featured by dictocrats lead to discord? And why does the road in the opposite direction, featured by a free and self-responsible people, lead to concord? If these questions can be clearly answered, we'll know how to keep our house from being divided against itself. Our house will not fall but will stand!

The road to serfdom—socialism, the planned economy, the welfare state, call it what you will—is featured by millions of dictocrats, all at sixes and sevens, each trying to make over society in his image. In view of their dissimilarities, it is instructive to reflect on what dictocrats have in common:

- An unawareness of how little they know. Actually, not one of them has any more rightful claim to omniscience than you or I.
- Each thinks you and I would fare better were we carbon copies of him.
- Even though not one of them knows how to make a pencil, a rope, a pane of glass, an auto, or even a meal, each entertains no doubt that were he to direct the whole economy it would be improved.[1]

Examples of this politically applied know-it-all-ness are the socialized money system, the Post Office, socialized medicine, public housing, TVA, garbage disposal; as well

---

[1]See "The Miracle of a Meal" in *Let Freedom Reign* (Irvington, New York: The Foundation for Economic Education, Inc., 1969), pp. 42-49.

as enormous intrusions into farming, airlines, railroads, power and light; plus efforts to control hours, wages, rents, interest, prices—to name but a few among tens of thousands.

Merely note the mess we're in—the failures more apparent each day. And the discord! With millions of dictocrats advancing as many or more panaceas—all at odds—how could it be otherwise! I do not agree with a one of them nor does one of them agree, really, with any of the others.

We are on the wrong road and the discord cannot be corrected unless we change direction. Given socialism as the objective, we will have to learn that there is no right way to achieve the wrong goal. Why this assertion? All that the dictocrats can possibly do to modify their mistakes—many of which are apparent even to them—is to attempt something less bad. But not so bad is error still! Never can what's right be achieved in this manner. For confirmation, note the countless attempts to make a go of socialized mail and how the service worsens. Emerson gave us the explanation:

> Cause and effect, means and ends, seed and fruit, cannot be severed; for the effect already blooms in the cause, the end pre-exists in the means, the fruit in the seed.

The seed is socialism; the fruit has to be discord!

True, the seed is socialism but socialism itself is the effect of a still deeper cause. And this cause is a blindness, a stumbling block, a major root of discord. This root cause is not only difficult for anyone to grasp but a clear explanation of it—communicability—borders on the impossible. The reason? The truth of the matter gives the appearance of a contradiction. Here is another try at clarification.

Such truth as is perceived by man is disclosed to discrete

individuals—the you's and I's. No argument! However, he who does not see beyond this fact, regards his little private version of truth as on a par with truth itself—all wise! Each individual of the millions afflicted with this egomania—all dictocrats—assesses himself as *the* focal point of wisdom. *I know I know!* These millions are in constant tension—every assumed focal point of wisdom being at odds one with the other. Discord! Bastiat had this to say:

> Therefore, those schools of thought that start with the assumption that *men's interests are antagonistic to one another have never yet done anything to solve the problem except to eliminate liberty.* They are still trying to ascertain which, out of all the infinite forms that coercion can assume, is the right one, or indeed if there is any right one. And, if they ever do reach any agreement as to which form of coercion they prefer, there will still remain the final difficulty of getting all men everywhere to accept it freely.[2]

Very well! What does lie beyond the fact that such truth as man perceives is disclosed to discrete individuals? In what "wild blue yonder," as the Air Force song has it, is wisdom to be found? If not in you or me, where, for heaven's sake? The answer: In all of us, near and far, past and present! It is an agglomeration of all inventions, discoveries, insights, intuitive flashes, think-of-that's since the dawn of consciousness, the chaff sieved from the seed by human experience. In a word, it is the overall luminosity—the wisdom not of any discrete individual but of the free and unfettered market.

I have attempted to explain—perhaps all too briefly—the way of life that leads to discord. What then is the way of life

[2]*Economic Harmonies* by Frederic Bastiat (Irvington-on-Hudson, New York: The Foundation for Economic Education, Inc., 1968), p. xxii.

that leads to harmony? It is every man pursuing his legitimate—intelligent—self-interest, that is, acting any way he pleases so long as his way does not impair the rights of others to be their creative selves. I quote Bastiat again because he so clearly saw the efficacy of this way:

> It is *practical,* for certainly no maxim is easier to put into practice than this: Let men labor, exchange, learn, band together, act and react upon one another, since in this way, according to the laws of Providence, there can result from their free and intelligent activity only *order, harmony, progress,* and all things that are good, and increasingly good, and still better, and better yet to infinite degree.[3]

Let us now reflect on the remedy, that is, how we may switch from the kind of actions that produce discord to the way of life that leads to concord. First of all, look not to a new Constitution or any other political or organizational gadgetry. Our original Constitution was but a recording of the leadership thinking of that time. The population, by and large, had no more grasp of that document and its significance than most people today; an appreciation of liberty and its meaning was as rare then as it is now. Observe that when the leadership thinking declines in quality, as it has, the Constitution becomes a mere scrap of paper. A new Constitution now, as is often suggested as a corrective for our present plight, would be no more than a recording of today's leadership "thinking." Heaven forbid!

The remedy is a coming to ourselves, an awakening, a *realization* of what goes on all about us—unnoticed and unap-

[3]*Ibid.*, p. xxx.

preciated. Some things come to our attention only when we are deprived of them. For instance, how many of us take note of or appreciate the air we breathe? Few indeed; that blessing, as so many others, is relegated to a taken-for-granted status. Similarly, with liberty. More or less unknowingly, liberty is a blessing to everyone, without which we would as surely perish as if we had no air to breathe.

A thought flashed to mind on a recent plane trip, having to do with one of the many sources of coercion. The captain, copilot, engineer, stewardesses—exceptionally pleasant folks—are labor union members. All of them receive above-market wages—the captain $57,000 annually—and below-market hours. They revel in their position. The thought that occurred to me? These people, with commendable exceptions, find it quite acceptable that their wage and hour "advantages" are due to the coercive power employed by their respective unions: give us what we demand or down go the airlines! There's no difference between this legally authorized brand of authoritarianism and the governmental kind: Washington says put up the fruits of your labor to pay farmers not to farm, for going to the moon, for the Gateway Arch, for urban renewal, on and on, or down go you—to jail.

Reflect on the millions of politicians and bureaucrats in government who, with many commendable exceptions, favor and exercise coercion and even more millions in labor unions who, again with many exceptions, also favor and exercise coercion. The aggregate coercion is unimaginable, coercion in every instance being the root of discord. Name an exception! Is it any wonder that discord rather than concord is dominant!

The seen and the unseen! These people who exercise coercion see only the "advantages" of their special privilege, of their coercion. They fail utterly to see that were it not for an enormous leakage of creative human energy—liberty—they wouldn't even exist to practice their legal plunder.

Return to the staff of the 747 jet. Were it not for liberty—creativity at work in spite of the enormous coercion—there would be no jet to fly, no food to serve, indeed, no passengers to accommodate. So far as humanity is concerned, a desolate earth! To repeat, liberty is as essential to survival as is the air we breathe.

The remedy is nothing less than an eye-opening performance, seeing that which is not seen. It is the seeing at once of a delusion and of a truth.

The delusion? It is a belief that the dictocrats' coercive tactics are responsible for life being as good as it still is. That which is seen!

The truth? That the free flowing of creative energy—liberty—is *the* source of human welfare. That which is not seen!

Concord can replace discord. It is only a matter of seeing. When seen, our house will no longer be divided against itself.

9

THE MISCHIEF OF MYTHS

> *Even when the facts are available, most people seem to prefer the legend and refuse to believe the truth when it in any way dislodges the myth.*
>
> —JOHN MASON BROWN

Mankind is more deeply swayed by myths than we are ready to concede, and these myths are a major source of conflict. The only remedy for this mischievous circumstance is the pursuit of truth. However difficult and uncommon the search for truth may be, it is the way to dislodge myths and to harmonize human relationships. Unpopular, of course; but a better way has never been discovered through a popularity poll.

An example of conflict stemming from a myth is the current "women's liberation" movement. This is featured by insistent demands for male-female equality in positions, pay, and other conditions. Indeed, the movement has gained so much momentum that women are employed in certain positions simply because they are women; competency is disregarded along with the employer's right to hire whomever he pleases. The number of men and women on this or that school faculty, for instance, must be equal, and there must be "equal pay for equal work." Wherever this notion is put into practice, conflict mounts. Conflict is a by-product of error.

The source of this particular error? There may be many, but probably the earliest myth was the account in Genesis: the first woman was "built up" from a rib of the first man. Women secondary and thus inferior to men! The literature during the past three thousand years is rife with pronouncements of female inferiority. And the current call is for instant equality.

Only the truth can dislodge this myth. The truth, as I see it, has two parts. First, women are no more equal to men than any woman is equal to any other woman or any man equal to any other man. Everything in the Cosmos—human, or snowflake, or whatever—is unique; things are neither identical nor equal; even for a single instant. Everything is one form or another of radiant energy, all in motion. Were all atoms equal the world would come to an end. Likewise, were all humans equal humanity would perish. Equality of men and women is a nonsensical ambition; it is, quite frankly, nothing but egalitarian politics.

Second, while women are outstandingly different, they are precisely as important as men. Wrote Bovee, "Next to God we are indebted to women, first for life itself, and then for making it worth having." The reverse is just as true. In a word, women are as essential to men as men are to women. Life is a unity-in-diversity composed of both men and women; the absence of either would spell nonexistence.

The answer! Dislodge the myth with those facts which seem so obvious. Let men and women find their place according to the merit of each individual person.

Before considering other illustrations concerning the mischief of myths in the politico-economic realm, let us note that the word myth has several connotations. On the one hand it refers to the fables of Zeus and his fellow Olympians—or the similar tales of other nations. On the other hand, the word myth is used in common speech as synonymous with error and deception. I am using myth here in this latter sense.

Michel de Montaigne (1533-1592), whose wise and fascinating writings may have had more influence on English literature than any other person and who I enjoy quoting favorably in most respects, nevertheless helped launch the pernicious myth that, "The profit of one man is the damage of another." (Essay XXI). This has come down to us as "any person's gain is someone else's loss."

Doubtless, this error had arisen in antiquity by countless unknown persons, those who had made no name for themselves. No effect! Montaigne, however, was famous, celebrated. If he were wise in many ways, why not assume his wisdom in all ways! To his credit, Montaigne inscribed on his coat of arms, *"Que sais-je?"*—What do I know? Yet, this humility on his part in no way deterred others from considering him wise in ways he was not, and in interpreting Essay XXI in ways Montaigne *might* not have intended. In any event, a terrible myth was nurtured having devastating international consequences not simply because of an error on the part of the author but more because of the error of popular genuflecting before prestige. It is becoming more obvious to me that it isn't so much what is said but, rather, who said it that gives birth and currency to myths.

Any person's gain is someone else's loss! While a myth, this cliche appears plausible to those who cannot or do not understand simple economics, and this includes numerous "economists." Assign prestigious authorship, and little if anything more is required for their acceptance of this nonsense! And this myth is, of course, utter nonsense to the few who are capable of sound economic thinking.

Conceded, in gambling one man's gain is another's loss. The dollar you win is the dollar I lose. But let us not correlate the production and exchange of goods and/or services with gambling. As farfetched would be to compare personal savings—capital formation—with thievery. Here we are concerned with willing exchange in the market, not a game of chance.

In the free and unfettered market the only way to gain is to perform a service for someone else—both traders gain—quite a switch from the pernicious myth! Actually, it would be difficult to find an individual who has not experienced this truth. When I swap my day's labor for your dollars, I value the dollars more than my labor and you value the labor more than your dollars or there would be no exchange. These gains—subjective judgments, of course—go on by the trillions, day in and day out. One doesn't need to be an economist to grasp this; merely keep the eyes open!

Observe how this my-gain-your-loss myth has taken on enormous proportions in today's world. Marxism is built around this same myth: the gain of employers and/or capitalists is at the expense of "laborers." This myth—"the labor theory of value"—is far from outmoded, unfortunately, but it has been completely demolished by such analytical thinkers as Menger, Böhm-Bawerk, Mises, and other more or less unknown individuals. What is the invalid theory—the myth—in Marxian terms? It declares that value is determined by the cost of production, and that production is by "wage earners," not by employers or capitalists.

The labor movement in the U.S.A., England, and several other countries is an extension of the same myth: invoke force to keep employers and capitalists from exploiting the "real" producers—"laborers," ranging from waiters to airline captains.

Keep in mind two points: (1) Marx and other big-name backers of this myth and (2) the devastating conflict that follows—as though there were *really* a conflict of interests!

A conflict of interests between those who work with their hands and those who work with their minds? Between brawn and brain, savers and spenders, employers and employees, producers and consumers? Or, as the Marxists have it, between capitalists and "laborers"? Of course not! The interests of these so-called categories—all of them—are in harmony, as much as are the true interests of men and women.

Conflict of interests originates when force—violence—is resorted to in order that some may feather their nests at the expense of others. In a word, Marxists—by whatever label—are the ones who attempt to live by pursuing a tired old myth, one that can be dislodged by grasping a few simple truths.

What are the simple truths? Any person who produces anything which is of value to anyone, whether with his hands or his mind, be he a gardener or an Edison, creates wealth. There are individuals who achieve more with their hands in a few days than others with their minds accomplish in a lifetime—and vice versa! All human beings who do creative work, in whatever manner or position, are at once employers and employees. A truck driver employs the makers of trucks who, in turn, employ truck drivers, architects, metallurgists, salesmen. I, for instance, am an employer and employee, a producer and consumer, a saver and a spender, a capitalist and a laborer, so-called categories to the contrary notwithstanding. There is no conflict when viewed aright, that is, when one is no longer victimized by the ancient myth. Rather, our interests are mutual—all in harmony!

To repeat, it seems obvious that myths, as well as truths, are brought to humanity and given currency by prestigious persons. What, then, about the few who have a grasp of free market truths and, at the same time, are lacking in prestige, fame? Hardly a big name among us! Wherein lies our hope? Have we no chance? My answer: We can make our chances!

Countless examples from the past and present might be cited as to how prestige is attained, that is, how we can make our chances. A single instance may suffice to make my point.

Jose Ortega y Gasset was an obscure Professor of Metaphysics at the University of Madrid. He wrote his first book in 1914: *Meditations on Quixote.*[1] For the next sixteen years he was a prolific writer of books and articles. Attention? Hardly any! "I am surprised," he wrote, "that not even those closest to me have the remotest notion of what I have thought and written." Assuredly, the nonprestigious Ortega!

Came 1932 and his *Revolt of the Masses.*[2] Immediately, it was a best seller in a score of languages—one of the most famous books of the century. Of a sudden, the prestigious

---

[1] *Meditations on Quixote* by Jose Ortega y Gasset (New York: W. W. Norton & Co., 1963).

[2] *Revolt of the Masses* by Jose Ortega y Gasset (New York: W. W. Norton & Co., 1932).

Ortega! What happened as a consequence of this new prestige? There was a publishers' rush for everything he had ever written—everything!

The lesson to be learned from Ortega's experience? Do as he did, namely, even when obscure—when no one is reading or listening—perform one's work with all the integrity and perfection one can command so that, if perchance later on millions of people become attentive, one can be proud to share what he has done. Let every act and thought of every day be performed as if one were to live with them forever.[3]

Finally, only now and then in the history of man does a devotee of freedom have Ortega's experience—millions attentive! To hope for such a miracle is to pull one's life out of focus. That's not where the eye should be cast.

Where, then? On the pursuit of what's right—the foundation of the only kind of prestige that matters. Whenever this becomes the focus of a man's life, *that's one more for our side!* Such exemplarity may persuade another one or two or more to emulate his actions. But, forget the numbers, for it's quality, not quantity, that can turn the American people again toward freedom. Possible? If only a relative few share my faith, it is certain!

---

[3]For a more detailed explanation of what I have learned from Ortega, see *To Free or Freeze* (Irvington-on-Hudson, N.Y.: The Foundation for Economic Education, Inc., 1972), pp. 162-168.

10

THE APPEAL OF ARROGANCE

When men are most sure and arrogant they are commonly most mistaken.

—DAVID HUME

Scan the biggest quotation book of all time and there are two quotes on "arrogance." As to its opposite—"humility"—there are seventy two! By and large, the same goes for other such books.

Why this wide margin? I suspect it's because famous writers, as ever so many others, have seen and felt the vice in arrogance as well as the virtue in humility. Further, arrogance is common, more or less, to nearly everyone, including yours truly. Thus, let's not be too harsh on ourselves by defaming arrogance! And, on the other hand, humility is so rare a trait in any of us that we attempt to identify with this virtue. In a word, divorce one's self from what we hold to be wrong and wed what we hold to be right—at least, make the effort. This may explain the margin.

Wrote Augustine, "The confession of evil works is the first beginning of good works." Therefore, should not one begin by confessing his own arrogance, an evil that strongly possesses most of mankind? The first step is to become acutely aware of how little one knows, and what a difficult stride that is! Two questions: (1) why difficult? and (2) why must it be taken?

A thorough realization that the awareness, perception, consciousness of any one of us is but an infinitesimal speck as related to Infinite Consciousness is indescribably difficult. Few, indeed, are those who have made the grade—who have arrived at true humility.

Why necessary? What is the moral command? Unless this step is taken and *fully* mastered, one will unavoidably proclaim and stand for things and/or ideas about which he knows absolutely nothing—a bigger I-AM or know-it-all than the facts warrant. This is haughtiness—arrogance! We shy away from identifying ourselves with this evil—observed far more in others than in ourselves.

In spite of my recognition of the above imperatives, I find it next to impossible to live in strict accordance with my own preachments, that is, not to think I know more than I really do. Suggested Nathaniel Crew, ". . . humility is a prudent care not to overvalue ourselves." Yes, I strive for this virtue but it seems, always, to be slightly beyond reach. In a word, I confess to traces of arrogance.

Here we are, nearly all of us, afflicted to some extent with arrogance, thinking that we know more than we do. Our kind are to be observed on every hand. And, interestingly, those who have attained a true humility are, so far as the general populace is concerned, more or less unknowns. The margin between arrogance and humility is much greater than in the quote books—except in reverse!

Now to my thesis, namely, the claim that arrogance has an appeal, that most people are attracted to rather than repulsed by this evil.

Example: We observe an individual who knows a great deal about some one thing. He knows he knows and so do we—the world's greatest portrait painter, for instance. How easy it is for him—likewise ourselves—to assume that he is an authority—is wise—on countless other matters. He is famous, wealthy, a genius. But how ingenious or all-wise is he, really?

Reflect on his limitations. He cannot grow the hemp from which his canvas is made, or construct the tools that harvest it, or make the weaver's loom or even operate it. His brushes and pigments are beyond his ken. And he hasn't the slightest idea how to mine the ore from which the saw is made that cuts the lumber that makes the frames for his masterpieces.

Unless this individual is so wise that he knows he knows not—a rarity—he will be overly impressed with himself and speak with "authority" on matters about which he knows nothing. Nothing whatsoever! Arrogance!

But more unfortunate than this individual's arrogance is the tendency of others to be attracted by his false presumption. It has an enormous appeal and can be avoided only by those who are aware that no person has more than an infinitesimal bit of wisdom or know-how. Why is arrogance so attractive? How come that so many fall easily into the trap of countless wiseacres? Perhaps it is because most of us prefer this "easy way" to its alternative: thinking for ourselves.

Also, we are market oriented. Ready-made goods by the millions—things made by others—are a boon to material welfare. Why not ready-made wisdom? Here there is a failure to distinguish between things that satisfy desires of the flesh and wisdom which is an accomplishment of the intellect. Acquiring wisdom is a do-it-yourself project. Surely, draw on the wisdom of others, but judge with careful scrutiny between bits of wisdom here and there and arrogance on the rampage. Everywhere!

The appeal of arrogance? Examples are prolific. Numerous outstanding generals have become the heads of their nations. Nor need the list be confined to Alexander the Great or Charlemagne or Napoleon. These persons overestimated their prowess and the citizens fell for it. The "reasoning?" Great at war, why not great at peace! Of outstanding strategists on the battlefield against enemies, why not expect outstanding statesmanship at home among friends? This is no less ridiculous than expecting the world's greatest portrait painter to reflect unquestioned wisdom in mathematics, astronomy, or baking bread!

For examples by the millions turn to the political front. Again, with rare and exemplary exceptions, these persons are aware of the general naivete of the citizenry. Their stock and trade? Demagoguery! Word artists! Actors who know not what they say! But this they do know: the appeal of their nonsense to those who think not for themselves. Their arrogance is unparalleled, as is its appeal—witness the electorate's favorable response. Listen to or read the daily grist. For the most part, it is but a repetition of the know-nots who pose as know-it-alls. *"When men are most sure and arrogant they are commonly most mistaken."* The mistakes are common—too common for common sense to prevail, unless—

Unless what? Unless there is an emerging humility, that

wonderful and necessary awareness of the minuscule state of knowledge and wisdom relative to the unknown. This, in my view, is the sole remedy for arrogance. And, it is not a problem of numbers. Our salvation rests exclusively on quality, that is, on the achievement of true humility—exemplarity. Fortunately, one or a few suffice to set an example. A tiny flame can kindle a huge blaze.

Interestingly, those who make the grade remain as unknowns except to those individuals here and there who are thinking for themselves, seeking light, wanting to know. And even in these cases, the ones who gain from those who are graced with humility seldom meet face to face. Nor does it matter. There is a radiation that flows between those who have something to share and those who seek. I know not *what* it is, only *that* it is. There *is* a Remnant in every society.

While writing this and seeking for a concluding thought, the following came from some unknown to me:

> The world is not going to the dogs. The human race is not doomed. Civilization is not going to crash. . . . Humanity is going through a difficult time, but humanity has gone through difficulties many times before in its long history, and has always come through, strengthened and purified. The Captain is on the bridge. God [Infinite Consciousness] is still in business. All that you have to do is to realize the Presence of God where trouble seems to be, *to do your nearest duty to the very best of your ability,* and keep an even mind until the storm is over.

Recognizing our finite awareness, perception, consciousness relative to Infinite Consciousness is the way to true humility, the overcoming of arrogance. The wiseacres will doubtless continue to expound and exhort, but we need not respond to their will. Have faith that the Captain is on the Bridge and that freedom will prevail. Beyond that, it behooves each individual to do his nearest duty to the very best of his ability.

11

SOCIALISM: THE OFFSPRING OF APATHY

He cared not for God or man.

—JOHN HEYWOOD

The only way I know to get at the roots of the mess we are in is to keep probing in every way until the last sustaining feeder is cut. And one of those feeders, I believe, is apathy.

The impulse to run the lives of others—the little-god syndrome—flourishes to the extent that the others are apathetic. To curb the dictocratic impulse calls for alertness, thinking for self, vigilance, virtuousness, a genuine care for God and man.

Imagine a debate on the subject: "Resolved that there should be no man-concocted restraints against the release of creative energy." The Affirmative debater is apathetic, listless. He has done no reading or thinking on the matter; indeed, he couldn't care less—all too typical. Does this not yield the case to the opposition? The person taking the Negative position can freely assert all the nonsense that plagues mankind, everything from the Divine Right of Kings to out-and-out Marxism. It's his day. Apathy is the seedbed of socialism!

Now, suppose the Affirmative is taken by one who truly believes in freedom. My late friend, James Rogers, was an excellent example. One evening he debated America's most celebrated socialist before an audience of 4,000, the socialist having a long winning record as a debater. But not on this occasion! Jim understood the freedom philosophy better than most of us and he was at once articulate, good natured, "quick on the trigger." He met each socialistic cliche with an incisive question which the socialist could only answer by contradicting himself. On they went for more than an hour, our friend smiling, the audience amused and enlightened, the socialist more and more frustrated, and eventually silent.

What this incident suggests to me is that the impulse to run the lives of others—the social problem plaguing mankind—can be rendered powerless, not through apathy, but through the energetic exercise of freedom.

Those who believe that we can be graced with abundance—material and/or intellectual—without effort are the pitiful victims of apathy and the ensuing dictatorship. Man's earthly purpose, I am confident, is to grow in awareness, perception, consciousness, that is, to harmonize as nearly as possible with Infinite Consciousness: God, Righteousness. It follows that apathy is the hell on earth from which all of us should seek escape.

The passion to domineer, the urge to cast others in one's image, is a common frailty. The lack of wisdom is its cause and socialism is its social consequence. Wisdom? Yes, the wiser one is the more aware he becomes of his own incapacity to rule others.

Medieval theologians are said to have discoursed on how many angels could dance on the head of a pin. Perhaps they were wiser than they knew. Reflect on the amount of information [angels?] in the chromosomes of a single human fertilized egg. It "is equivalent to about a thousand printed volumes of books, each as large as a volume of *The Encyclopedia Britannica.* This amount of coded instruction packed into the size of a *millionth of a pinhead* is the remarkable material which transmits information from parent to offspring to tell the next generation how to make a person."[1]

That passage was a great lesson in humility for me. Cast others in my image? Domineer? Out of the question! As Disraeli phrased the point, "To be conscious that you are ignorant is a great step to knowledge."

Yes, we do need seers, but not see-it-alls. For only those who see how minuscule is man's knowledge can see the vital necessity of everyone's acting creatively as he pleases—freedom from domination by see-it-alls. Man requires freedom to progress in awareness, perception, consciousness—his earthly purpose!

Parenthetically, I have reservations about debate as an effective educational tactic.[2] And with reference to the performance by James Rogers, I expect he had no more potentiality than countless others; *he merely did more with what*

---

[1]From a paper, "Some Biological Considerations of Ethics," presented at Massachusetts Institute of Technology by Hudson Hoagland.

[2]For an explanation, see *Then Truth Will Out* (Irvington, N.Y.: The Foundation for Economic Education, Inc., 1971), pp. 125-130.

he had! What distinguished him from the mill run of citizens was his awareness of the vast unknown and an insatiable urge for excellence. He was not apathetic about freedom.

Were the U.S.A. to be graced with individuals thus oriented, the domineering trait would not necessarily be erased from the souls of men but much of it would be effectively challenged and silenced. The darkness of socialistic error, regardless of its volume, cannot prevail against the overwhelming light of freedom and truth. So, let us overcome apathy with alertness, thinking for self, vigilance, virtuousness, and a genuine care for God and man.

- *Alertness* involves an awakening, an awareness of the hidden potentialities to be discovered in each of us and put to full use.
- *Thinking for self* is the only kind of thinking there is. It is to understand and absorb and put to use in one's own life all worthy thoughts, from whatever source.
- *Vigilance* is to guard against the domineering trait in self and in others, that creative human energy may freely flow.
- *Virtuousness* means respectful adherence to such guidelines as integrity, humility, justice, charity.
- *A genuine care for God and man* is to seek righteousness in our lives and a reverence toward others, an interdependence effectuated through freedom.

Are these wondrous opposites of apathy too much to expect, too difficult to attain? Certainly they are well within the range of any serious aspirant. Think of the rewards to the victors! They are twofold: the downfall of socialism, meaning the reign of liberty, plus each victor's approximation of his or her earthly purpose!

12
SOCIALISM GROWS LIKE WEEDS

Nature and certainty are very hard to come at, and infallibility is mere vanity and pretense.

—**MARCUS AURELIUS**

What can be made of this great Stoic's observation? By "nature and certainty" he meant nothing less than Truth, and this is indeed hard to come by! It's like reaching for a star moving in outer space at the speed of light. Or finite minds striving to grasp Infinite Consciousness! Nonetheless, one must try to approach Truth, though it can never be wholly perceived. The more Truth one discovers, the more there is to discover.

Infallibility is appropriately described as "mere vanity and pretense." There is no such human quality as infallibility. The illusion of infallibility is spawned by the most pronounced of all human errors: an ignorance of how little one knows; it is the little-god syndrome! As Jacques Barzun so eloquently phrased the reason for this all-too-common trait:

> Intellect deteriorates after every surrender to folly: unless we consciously resist, the nonsense does not pass by us but into us.[1]

Now to my analogy. Suppose the world were populated by two-legged animals having no knowledge of soil cultivation, only feeding on whatever grows. Productive discernment nil! The consequence? All the fertile land on the face of the earth, except nature's wonderful forests, would be covered with weeds, a weed being defined as "any undesired, *uncultivated* plant that grows in profusion so as to crowd out a *desired* crop." In other words, in the absence of any intelligent, productive cultivators of the soil, a weed patch!

Analogous to weeds is human error. In what way? In the absence of intelligent self-interest—the virtues that can, should, and are supposed to grace mankind—we would be steeped in error, errors being all *undesired* fallacies that spread in profusion so as to crowd out what is good and true. When not discerned, error breeds error, endlessly! Unless we individually and *consciously* resist, the nonsense will not pass us by but into us. Folly will be the lot of mankind—world-wide, as today.

What is the error here at issue, the error that breeds error? It is planned chaos for which there have been and are numerous labels: feudalism, egalitarianism, mercantilism, fascism, communism, Fabianism, the planned economy, the welfare state, and so on. The feature common to every one

---

[1]*The House of Intellect* by Jacques Barzun (New York: Harper & Bros., 1959), p. 222.

of these? Authoritarianism—dictocrats running our lives!

Regardless of labels, I call the whole kit and caboodle "socialism" as the Russians do, the U.S.S.R. being but an abbreviation for Union of Soviet *Socialist* Republics. There follows my definition of socialism as it is practiced not only in the U.S.S.R. but to a larger and larger extent in the U.S.A.:

> Socialism is the state ownership and control of the *means* of production (the planned economy) and the state ownership and control of the *results* of production (the welfare state).

In what manner does our socialism differ from the Russian brand! There are some differences in organizational detail between a U.S.S.R. commissar and a U.S.A. dictocrat. But each suffers the error of know-it-all-ness, that is, "I know how to run your life better than you do; leave your mortal moment to infallible me." Except for the phrasing, this is their sales pitch; they sincerely believe this to be their role and are encouraged in so believing by the millions of people who, shying away from self-responsibility, are looking for shepherds and sheep dogs.

Of course, the fact is that no dictocrat knows how to run the life of any human being, let alone the lives of millions. Anyone who grasps the error of the master-slave relationship should see this as self-evident.

Daily we observe the dictocrats themselves acknowledging that such and such a plan has not come up to their expectations. Lacking the capacity to recognize their know-nothingness in this respect, and spurred on by a passion to rule, do they repeal the error? No, they leave it on the statute books *and add another and another, endlessly!*

All I am trying to point out is that error, unless discerned, breeds error, as weeds breed weeds. These errors proliferate in our 100,000 governments—federal, state, and local. Millions of errors backed by force—planned chaos. Such is the nature of the mess we are in.

What should we do? Well, this is no time to throw up our hands in despair and say in effect, "The free society is a goner!" Such surrender to folly suggests that we confine our part to watching the mobs go by—the dictocrats and their followers—and be content with no more correction of the mess we're in than to glory in "I told you so!" Really, is this any less nonsense than that which is declaimed? The nonsense has not passed by such persons but into them.

It is this lethargy—"asleep at the switch"—that is overcoming us. What goes on for the most part is remindful of arsonists who have set fire to a house. "The house is a goner," say the many. And it is a goner if there be no exception to such folly. How save the house? Let a few with their equipment consciously resist. Out goes the fire!

How consciously resist? Good equipment which, in the intellectual realm, includes:

- A recognition of socialism in all of its forms and disguises and an ability simply to explain its fallacies.
- An ever-improving understanding and explanation of how the free market, private ownership, limited government way of life works its wonders.
- Exemplarity in word and deed—morally above all, for freedom is a moral achievement.
- Never say die; have faith; believe that out of the current mess can and will emerge the better ideas for a better life.

Yes, error breeds error as weeds breed weeds. But as cultivators of the soil bring desired crops in their stead, so do cultivated minds replace error with what's good and true. Consciously resist and be graced with freedom which permits each and every citizen to become his own creative self!

13

THE RISE AND FALL OF SELF-RELIANCE

Trust thyself: every heart vibrates to that iron string. Accept the place the divine providence has found for you.

—**EMERSON**

The place divine providence has found for each individual attests to the uniqueness of that person. Trust thyself merely means to pursue and perfect one's own creative talents, whatever they are. This is the iron string of self-interest to which each heart is naturally attuned, however poorly one understands the tune or acts out of harmony with it. Why does man thus deviate? There may be many reasons, but chief among them must be the coercive forces that suppress and atrophy self-reliance.

Self-reliance has graced ever so many individuals here and there during the span of history. However, until less than 200 years ago, these were rare souls relative to the populations in which they lived. Serfdom, feudalism, mercantilism, and other forms of slavery held the masses at bay—deadened rather than enlivened this stalwart quality. For the millions, it was reliance on others rather than self. So-called civilizations of the past, with minor exceptions, lacked any human sparkle.[1]

It was in this land of ours that self-reliance rose to its all-time sparkling heights. It is necessary that we know why in order to understand its decay.

Briefly, the American miracle had its genesis in three political documents: The Declaration of Independence, the Constitution, and the Bill of Rights.

1. The Declaration set the stage by declaring that men's rights to life and liberty are endowed by the Creator. A historical first, this unseated government as the endower of those rights.
2. The Constitution and the Bill of Rights more severely limited government than government had ever before been limited. In essence, these documents forbade government to interfere with creative and productive activities—these being the exclusive prerogative of the individual citizens.

There were two remarkable benefits that flowed from this unprecedented limitation of government.

1. When government is limited, as in our original design, to invoking a common justice, to inhibiting the destructive actions of men, to keeping the peace, no one turned to it for security, welfare, or prosperity. Why? Thus limited, it had nothing on hand to dispense nor did it have the power to take from some and give to others. To whom, then, did the citizen turn? To self! There de-

[1]Florence, during the reign of Lorenzo the Magnificent, was one such exception. See *The Medici* by G. F. Young (New York: Modern Library).

veloped among Americans a quality of character that Emerson referred to as "self-reliance." All over the world Americans gained the reputation of being a self-reliant people.

2. With government thus limited, there was, for the first time in history, no organized force standing against the release of creative energies. What happened? The greatest outburst of creative energy ever known!

The foundation of this self-reliance which featured the American miracle? No question about it to my way of thinking: the spiritual antecedent; namely, that men—all men, the millions—are endowed by the Creator (and not by the government!) with unalienable rights to life and liberty.

In previous "civilizations" where only the few were graced with self-reliance, creativity remained in limbo. When only the monarch, the lord of the manor, the slavemaster—one among thousands—is self-reliant, there is strikingly little generative force, compared to the American miracle. No sparkle, no get-up-and-go! These primitive civilizations recognized no fall from self-reliance simply because they had risen to no heights from which to fall. Thus, when commenting on the decline and fall of this rare and important human quality, I shall confine my observations to the U.S.A. where it had its greatest rise, making the fall easy to identify.

When an individual is self-reliant—relies on self rather than others—he is a whole person; the very essence of his being is encased within him rather than scattered to the four winds. In such an instance, the iron string of self-interest is at work full force, to which each heart is naturally attuned. All the creativity that is within one flows forth.

In the more of less primitive civilizations of yesterday's and today's world, where only one among countless thousands is self-reliant, creativity is hardly noticeable—it barely exists. Now, create a climate of freedom as was intended under the U.S. Constitution, emphasizing self-reliance and tapping the creativity of the millions, and we have the simple explanation of the American miracle—the unprecedented outburst of creative energy. In such an environment, creativity was multiplied by thousands times countless thousands!

A mere sampling: A 12 year-old newsboy on a train, a waif by the name of Tom, became one of the greatest inventive geniuses of all time. Thomas Alva Edison an isolated instance of creativity bursting out of the common man? Indeed, not! An army officer fathered photography; a bookbinder's clerk, the electric motor; a portrait painter, the telegraph; a farmer, the typewriter; a poet, the sewing machine; a cabinetmaker, the cotton gin; a coal miner, the locomotive. No one can more than guess at the millions of similar outcroppings of creativity.

As we reflect on the decline of self-reliance, it seems obvious that whenever an individual passes the responsibility for self over to another, or permits the government to assume the responsibility for his livelihood, *that person loses the very essence of his being;* self-reliance cannot flower in the absence of self-responsibility. Each is dependent on the other. Creativity is deadened in those thus afflicted, whether they relinquished responsibility voluntarily or were compelled to do so. The iron string is broken and broken strings do not vibrate; creativity no longer flows from such persons.

A distressing thought to bear in mind is that creativity no more flows from the keepers than from the kept. Who are the kept? Those receiving food stamps approximate 16,000,000.

Countless other schemes such as unemployment insurance—getting paid not to work—make it impossible accurately to assess the number of those who are now wards of the state: the kept. These persons are no longer self-reliant and thus are noncreative and they comprise a strikingly large percentage of the population. No Edisons among them!

What about the keepers? Who are they? They are that part of the vast army of government employees—federal, state, and local—beyond those few who perform its legitimate function. They are the ones who employ coercive force not only to take from some persons and redistribute to others, but also to prescribe how businessmen and other owners may use and price their own property. How many keepers? Oddly enough, there are about as many of these keepers as there are recipients of food stamps—approximately 16,000,000. These keepers are no more self-reliant than the kept, for both depend upon what is taken from producers.

While the keepers are neither self-reliant nor creative, there is no denying that they are inventive. True, they do not invent goods and services by which citizens live and prosper; they invent clever schemes to acquire possession of goods and services from producers. They are ingenious word artists, so good at framing plausibilities and cliches that most people are "taken in."

Is it not self-evident that these keepers who devote their "thinking" exclusively to running the lives of others give no heed to the perfection of their lives? In a word, we must never expect creativity from any of those who haven't taken the first step in wisdom, namely, in knowing that they know not. No Edisons among the keepers, any more than among the kept!

Here, however, is the most distressing fact of all: *These unwise keepers are trying to usurp the role of the Creator; they presume to be the endowers of human rights.*

How many regulatory agencies do we have staffed by keepers? There are about 100,000 governments in the U.S.A., each of which has countless agencies controlling about every aspect of life one can imagine. No one knows all the controls. Indeed, no one could know were he to spend a lifetime trying to find the answer. In any event, it is these controls that account for the mess we're in, ranging all the way from upside-down education, to surpluses and shortages, to unemployment, to inflation, to the energy crisis, on and on. All of this is brought about by the keepers, those who presume themselves to be the endowers of human rights.

Two questions need an answer. First, in all this darkness, with all these ridiculous controls, how can our situation be no worse than it is? With self-reliance and creativity deadened in so many of us—the keepers and the kept—from whence come the self-reliance and creativity that keep our economy from total decadence and collapse? There has to be an explanation. Here is mine: Our sustenance comes from a few individuals—a very small percentage of the population—in whom these stalwart qualities will not down. They are the cream of the crop, as we say. They're of that stout stock from whom came the self-reliance and creativity which featured America's finest hour.

Looking out for self, developing one's talents, is a social duty, contrary to popular opinion. As William Graham Sumner phrased this truth, ". . . making the most of one's self . . . is not a separate thing from filling one's place in society, but the two are one, and the latter is accomplished when the former is done." Our politico-economic saviours today are the inheritors of this iron string of enlightened self-interest—mostly unknown, but self-reliant and creative giants, none-theless.

The second question: What are *we* to do about this discouraging trend, this flight, from self-reliance and creativity? We collectively cannot do anything except as the challenge is faced individually, in the first person, singular: What can *I* do about it?

Emerson gives me my guideline: Trust myself by pursuing and perfecting such creative talents as I possess. See that my heart vibrates to that iron string of enlightened self-interest. These stalwart qualities cannot be taught; they can only be caught. This presupposes individuals so advanced in self-reliance and creativity that it becomes contagious. Exemplarity, and that alone, is the answer!

14

THANK GOD FOR THE MESS WE'RE IN

Cause and effect, means and ends, seed and fruit, cannot be severed; for the effect already blooms in the cause, the end pre-exists in the means, the fruit in the seed.

—EMERSON

There is a reason for our mess. We are now reaping the bitter harvest of the poisonous seed sowed intermittently during the past. We are experiencing bad effects whose causation can be traced to the employment of wrong means. We suffer the natural consequences of our folly, which proves once again that the universe is rational. To state this in another way, if improper methods *did not* lead to failures, we would really have a problem. As it is, we need only take our heads out of the sand to see clearly that interventionism not only has failed to provide the promised something-for-nothing but has led to all sorts of undesirable consequences.

Heads in the sand! I refer to those who do no more than lament the mess we are in; all they "think" about is whether they can survive it. Though greatly puzzled, they fail to get the message the mess is meant to convey. Indeed, many are just beginning to realize that we are moving toward disaster, even though we have been on a wrong heading for decades.

Why then do I thank God for the mess we're in? Simply because the mess is sending up signals—messages loud and clear—that our past is filled with errors which inexorably produced their evil results. The consequences we suffer now were caused by past mistakes, and we need to know what wrong actions are responsible for these bad effects. The fact is, we are being graced with warnings which, when and if read aright, can lead to our salvation. That's why I thank God!

Bearing in mind that what happens has an instruction peculiarly its own and that there is something good in everything bad, let us try to find the lesson. Our past is filled not only with moral but politico-economic errors, and our present likewise. How are we to identify these wrong actions and find the right ones, that is, how expose the fallacies of state interventionism and reveal the merits of human liberty as related to the interest and benefit of every one of us?

When liberty prevails, every individual in the entire population is free to bring *persons* and other scarce resources into complementary and workable combinations. Reflect on our varied talents. If we approach the matter properly, we come to note our own lack of most of the talents known to man. I, for instance, could no more bring musicians and instruments together to form an orchestra than I could bring technicians and tools together to release atomic energy or to deliver the human voice at the speed of light. But look around; there are millions who can and do bring individuals and other resources into association that render a fantastic service of all sorts to

King Consumer. And, when liberty prevails so does competition, a constructive force that assures that the efficient servants rise to serve all of us better.

When liberty prevails, there are in the U.S.A. not less than 130,000,000 adults free to release their greatly varied and *unique* creative energies. The aggregate of these energies—the bringing into combination of *things* and *persons* —is beyond the power of anyone to even imagine, let alone measure.

Let us now observe what happens to these sources of creative energy when the state regulates and controls them. What are the consequences when organized physical force—government—controls our creativity, our varied and unique potentialities? To accurately observe and appraise these consequences is to discover the errors—moral and economic—which account for the mess we are in. And the task is to free ourselves from these malpractices.

Suppose that we have found an outstanding individual who has all the degrees and honors mankind has ever bestowed on anyone. How easy to conclude that we, the ordinary consumers, would fare far better than we do now by our own choices, if only we would yield instead to his "wisdom." Assume next that he is given the power to impose his will only on a single person: You. The power to cast you in his image! Instantly, two individuals have become noncreative—you and he!

It is obvious why this dictocratic action would abolish your creativity—you have become but an image of him. But why the "great" one? How does this diminish his creativity? Whatever effort he devotes to lording it over you is effort he cannot exercise creatively. No one can, at one and the same time, be a dictocrat and a practitioner of liberty. *These roles are mutually exclusive.* So, we have here a small-scale model of the mess.

From this model proceed to the prevailing situation in the U.S.A. We have some 100,000 governments—federal, state, and local—and about 16,000,000 on the payrolls. An enormous percentage of these persons—little folks, even as you and I—are not just telling a single person what to do but commanding millions of us as to what to produce, what and with whom to exchange, what our money is worth; they dictate hours of labor, wages, what our children must study; on and on and on, even to seat belts.

Summarized, these 16,000,000 with some notable exceptions—those who are not dictocrats—have not only removed themselves from the nation's 130,000,000 potential entrepreneurs but, far worse, they have frustrated, to a marked extent, the morals and the creativity of the citizenry.

As a result of this governmental intervention, the varied talents and the uniqueness of each citizen are more or less imprisoned. Add to this the dictatorial, coercive powers extended to labor unions on an enormous scale and, on a lesser scale, to farmers, businessmen, educators, welfare agencies and others.[1] This is a sketch of the mess we are in.

To repeat, when liberty prevails, all are free to bring things and people into workable combinations to the betterment of all, the policeman included. But when the police and their subsidized minions regulate and control, a do-as-I-say-or-else action replaces, to a great extent, the *bringing* to-

[1]If governments at all levels are taking over 40 per cent of our earned incomes, then perhaps we should recognize that over 40 per cent of us are acting as policemen rather than as productive, creative, peaceful producers of goods and services.

gether actions of free and creative people, and to the detriment of all.

Why the qualifying term, "to a great extent"? Why not a total breakdown? The idea and practice of liberty is not that easily overcome. We are born to be free. Having had many experiences with liberty during the past two centuries, citizens will course their way around and through the dictatorial edicts; they'll find loopholes—become schemers, evaders. This ingenuity, though debilitating, explains why the mess is not as bad as it might otherwise be; why we continue to live in spite of the mess; why, despite mass killings, millions lived in Nazi Germany and Communist Russia. A fortuitous leakage of creative human energy! As Lord Macaulay observed in 1839:

> It has often been found that profuse expenditures, heavy taxation, absurd commercial restrictions, corrupt tribunals, disastrous wars, seditions, persecutions, conflagrations, inundations, have not been able to destroy capital so fast as the exertions of private citizens have been able to create it.[2]

The signals are loud and clear—far too numerous to recount. The messages are that every one of these evils we now experience are but consequences of past and present errors. As Emerson so wisely pointed out, "Cause and effect cannot be severed." We must work on the causes rather than the effects if we would repair our ways!

Let me conclude by calling attention to but one signal, a warning that is fretting millions of concerned people all over

---

[2]See Chapter III in Macaulay's *The History of England* (New York: E. P. Dutton, 1934), p. 217.

the world: the rapid decline in the purchasing power of the dollar. The cause? Inflation! Its causes? Excessive governmental expenditures which in turn are caused by people from all walks of life running to government for every conceivable kind of succor—people feathering their own nests at the expense of others. The remedy? Remove the causes.[3]

In any event, I thank God for the mess we're in and its timely warning that we must change our course to avert disaster.

---

[3]If interested in a more detailed explanation, see my "How to Stop Inflation," *The Freeman,* November 1973.

15

WRINGING OUT THE MESS

The history of liberty is a history of the limitation of governmental power, not the increase of it.

—WOODROW WILSON

Our political economy is a mess: inflation, unemployment, bad debts, shortages, surpluses, controls, crime—the list goes on—the chickens of intervention come home to roost. There are millions of Americans today who are awake to this distressing fact. What should be done? A vast majority only bemoan our plight, wring their hands in grief, and let it go at that. The tragedy is less in the mess than in this lethargy! Let me pose what may be a helpful analogy.

A sponge will sop up an awful lot of mess. But when the sponge becomes saturated, the sponge itself is a mess. How to make it useful again? Not by wringing our hands in grief but by *wringing the mess out of it!*

The mess we face today has a message, a purpose. If we only moan and wring our hands in lethargy, the mess will continue—until more individuals than now eventually get the message. So, what is the purpose? What should we do? Horace, the Roman poet of 20 centuries ago, wrote:

> Adversity has the effect of eliciting talents which in prosperous circumstances would have lain dormant.

The purpose of this mess—adversity—is to elicit talents which presently lie dormant. Why dormant? There are at least two reasons. The first is that Americans have experienced the greatest era of prosperity in the world's history. True, the mess is fulfilling its purpose, that is, bringing forth the required talents in some instances. By and large, however, our situation resembles what George Horne once described:

> Prosperity too often has the same effect on its possessor, as a calm at sea has on the Dutch mariner, who frequently, it is said, in these circumstances, ties up the rudder, gets drunk and goes to sleep.

Yes, our unprecedented prosperity has put most Americans to sleep. Why then are they not awakened by inflation and all the other chickens of intervention that have come home to roost? Why does not this adversity elicit the talents and serve the purpose it should? The answer lies in the second reason, in the more or less unseen. To return to my analogy, we are the beneficiaries of a politico-economic sponge so efficient in soaking up messes that most citizens are unaware that there is a mess. Americans, today, are still more prosperous than have been the people of any other place or time. And all because of a better sponge than has heretofore existed!

What is this remarkable politico-economic sponge? It is the nearest approximation to the free and unfettered market any nation has ever experienced. It is featured by freedom to produce and exchange, to travel, to retain the fruits of one's own labor, private ownership, a fair field and no favor, no man-concocted restraints against the release of creative human energy. In other words, it is human action when government is limited to inhibiting destructive behavior, invoking a common justice—keeping the peace.

Our near approach to the freedom ideal explains America's unprecedented outburst of productivity, thus prosperity. All productivity—no exception—stems from the releasing, freeing of creative energy. Coercive or dictatorial direction—"management"—diverts the course of productive efforts and eventually discourages further production.

This assertion is unbelievable to most people for they observe productivity in Russia, for instance, where dictatorship reigns. At home, they see the socialistic post office delivering mail, or TVA generating and distributing electricity, and so on. So, how can such a contention as mine be right? Overlooked is the fact that all of these are relative failures. For example, the non-whites in North Carolina alone own more automobiles than all the people in Russia; we deliver the human voice fantastically more efficiently than government delivers mail.

However, the fact that so often escapes notice is that all so-called government productivity, in Russia or at home, can be accounted for *exclusively* by a leakage of creative energy—energy not contained by authority. If dictatorship were totally effective, that is, if government authority were supreme—Do as we say!—all people would perish. Productivity in Russia, such as it is, or mail delivery at home, is in spite, not because, of the coercive intervention.

The traits we inherit stem largely from ancestors unknown, and we become complacent and lethargic about that heritage. Likewise, we accept our remarkable politico-economic sponge, acting in response to it without fully understanding what it is.

Our heritage is freedom and regardless of how rapidly the interventions increase we still act to a remarkable extent as free men. We inherited the trait and, unaware of this fact, *we give it no credit!* Reflect on the observation by Lord Macaulay cited in the previous chapter.

Dr. Benjamin Rogge, as a visiting professor in Brazil in 1956, asked some business leaders how they could be so successful in the light of the inflation and other government interventions. They replied, "We do our work at night while the politicians sleep."

In the U.S.A. today, the politicians seldom sleep. For the most part—there are a few remarkable exceptions—they are on an interventionist rampage. So our producers—acting by instinct—manage to course their way through and around the interventions. There is an unbelievable and generally unrecognized momentum at work which is our politico-economic salvation—*for the time being!* It is this response to our heritage of freedom, acting as free men more or less unknowingly, that accounts for how well we are getting along in spite of inflation and all the nonsensical interventions. It is this vestige of freedom and this alone that sops up the mess we are in!

For the time being! When is the deadline? Who knows! The determining factor is an awakening as to what our inherited trait really is, the trait that is sopping up the mess more or less without our knowing it: *individual liberty.* Short of this, our sponge will become too saturated for a mere inherited trait to wring the mess out of it. It's this or else!

Woodrow Wilson pinpointed the truth in this matter: "The

history of liberty is a history of *limitations of governmental power,* not the increase of it." He, then, saw the light that we must see.

A bit more to the question, how then did our countrymen get off the track? What slippage in—or absence of—thinking accounted for a switch from limited to unlimited government? While not certain, I have a suspicion that seems worth sharing. It goes as follows:

1. A vast majority, even in our heyday of freedom, hadn't the vaguest idea as to why this outburst of creativity. Like our contemporaries, they were totally unaware of any relationship between the fact that hardly any organized force stood against honest enterprise and the ensuing miracle.
2. With rare exceptions, Americans have seen only surface appearances: organized force and the miracle. Being unaware of true cause and noting only effect, they fall easy victims to claims by political office seekers, namely, that government—organized force—performs miracles of whatever sort. The chant of our time—millions upon millions of voices—what a wondrous and omniscient agency of society government is!
3. The gruesome point: *It seems to work!* Organized force—government—passes itself off as the worker of miracles in whatever area. Thus, the insistence that all enterprise be directed by government, be it education or mail delivery or any other business activity.

What is your role and mine? See that light ourselves, dim as it is, and become enlightened. This is our only way to wring out the mess. Remember, "There is not enough darkness in the whole world to put out the light of one wee candle."

16

POLICE: FRIEND OR FOE?

Government is not reason, it is not eloquence—it is force. Like fire it is a dangerous servant and a fearful master; never for a moment should it be left to irresponsible action.

—GEORGE WASHINGTON

Woodrow Wilson, in his book, *The State,* also identifies government with force: "Government, in its last analysis, is organized force." Stated very simply, a government issues edicts—laws—which are backed by a constabulary or policemen. Obey, or suffer the consequences! Other agencies or persons must rely on attraction, service rendered, peaceful persuasion.

It is beginning to dawn on me that we who believe in and are spokesmen for what we have called "limited government" have been using that term in vain. Why the suspicion? Again, hear Woodrow Wilson:

No man ever saw the people of whom he forms a part. No man ever saw a government. I live in the midst of the *Gov-*

> *ernment of the United States.* I never saw the Government of the United States.

In a word, we have been sponsoring, arguing for, trying to explain something no one ever saw—trying to make the case for an unperceived abstraction!

In the interest of better communication, why not use a term that is consonant with what organized force really is: *the police.* All of us, from youngsters to oldsters, have seen policemen. Woodrow Wilson, for instance, never saw government but he saw policemen, one of them in the mirror—a Chief of Police. So let us try that image of limited government —the police— to better present our freedom point of view.

The question is this: Are our policemen—local, state, and national—friends or foes? This, I believe, can be resolved by assessing their countless actions as related to justice and injustice. They are friends when supporting justice and foes when inflicting injustices.

Here is my conclusion at the outset: When the police serve as an agency of justice, we should in all good conscience regard the agency as a friend. But when the police power becomes an instrument of injustice we should look upon it as a foe; for then it is a political device that contributes toward rather than deters social chaos. Above all, let us bear in mind that the police force is but an agency or an instrument of ours, and that ours is the responsibility to keep it a friendly agency of justice rather than a foe of mankind.

Wrote Edmund Burke: "Whenever a separation is made between liberty and justice, neither, in my opinion, is safe." I side with Burke: Liberty and justice are inseparably linked! So, what is liberty? It is the "pursuing of our own good in our own way, so long as we do not attempt to deprive others of theirs, or impede their efforts to obtain it." My phrasing: No man-concocted restraints against the release of creative human energy.

Let me catalogue a few instances where the police behave as a foe and try to explain how the agency could serve as a friend instead.

Inflation: When the agency dilutes the medium of exchange it is a foe, precisely as if every policeman in the U.S.A. were engaged in counterfeiting. Foe? If the money supply continues to escalate at the rate since 1938—from about $35 billion to $280 billion—the supply by the year 2000 will be one and one-half trillion dollars. Savings, insurance, bonds, and other such assets wouldn't then be worth a plugged nickel. Here is a separation of liberty and justice.

How can the police agency become a friend? Remove the cause of inflation: excessive police expenditures. For it is an observed fact that whenever the costs of the police power rise beyond that point where it is no longer politically expedient to defray its costs by direct tax levies, such agencies resort to inflation as a means of making up the deficit. Inflation syphons private property into the coffers of the police. Let the police power do only what police are supposed to do: Invoke a common justice and keep the peace! That would be a big step toward liberty and friendship.

Food stamps: a perfect example of the police agency as foe! In 1965 the cost of the food stamp program was $85.5 million. This year it will approximate $7.2 billion—up 8,400 per cent in ten years—with 16,000,000 people riding this gravy train, feeding at the public trough. Where is this and similar plundering schemes of the police force taking us? To a situation of all parasites and no hosts—the rich becoming poor and the poor poorer. Liberty and justice separated!

The light shed by this police injustice? Allow everyone maximum opportunity to become self-responsible. It is as unjust for the police to forcibly take from some and give to others as it would be for me to rob you to aid a person who is the object of my pity. What about instances of distress? Rely on the practice of Judeo-Christian charity. Were the police not pre-empting this role, true personal charity would be more than sufficient. For another step toward liberty and justice, let us relieve the policeman of this highly questionable activity.

Social Security: Why should every person engaged in "covered employment" be compelled to contribute 11.7 per cent of the first $13,200 of his annual earnings to this huge "policemen's benevolence fund"? For the benefit of those already retired? For a chance to draw from the fund if and when he reaches 65 and retires from "covered employment"? Is it justice to force everyone to contribute to this "fund for the future" regardless of the individual's present needs and circumstances or of his own ideas about how best to save and invest his property?

What should a friendly policeman do in this regard? Why not ask that he protect and defend the right of each of us to buy as much or as little insurance as he wants from whomever is willing to supply it? And if either party attempts to defraud the other, let the policeman then intervene as an agent of justice.

Price controls: The police are foes when they control the price of commodities, rent, interest, wages or permit control by labor or business or whoever. Prices are expressions of value judgments. No policeman or anyone else can determine the value of this or that for you or me. Value is always a subjective determination. When the policeman tells you what price you must pay or at what price you must sell, he is, in effect, forcing you to buy or sell contrary to your wishes; in other words, he is controlling you. All attempts at price control have failed; the results have been surpluses and shortages and economic chaos. People control is rank injustice.

The friendly policemen let prices be determined in the free and unfettered market, that is, by supply and demand. Liberty and justice!

Paying farmers not to farm: a foe to consumers—who pay more; a foe to taxpayers—who keep less; a foe to the farmers themselves—who degenerate into plunderers.

The friendly way? Be done, "lock, stock, and barrel," with this silly blockage of the market. Restore liberty and justice!

Police-type education: This is featured by three forms of police coercion: (1) compulsory attendance, (2) police dictated curricula, and (3) the forcible collection of the wherewithal to pay the enormous bill. The police have no more place in education than in religion. In my view, police "education" has been one of the greatest errors in American history and this fact is becoming more and more evident with each passing year. The collectivistic jargon issuing from classrooms accounts, in no small measure, for collectivistic practices in all walks of life. Foes!

What then would be friendly? Get the police out of education except to identify any and all misrepresentation, and impose appropriate penalties! Leave education—as we leave religion—to citizens acting freely, cooperatively, competitively, privately, voluntarily. Education is a voluntary taking of ideas freely offered by others, not a police process of stuffing information into a captive audience. The police who side with this view are friends and the upholders of liberty and justice as related to education.

Why give more examples of a list virtually endless? These few specimens—a mere sampling—may suffice to demonstrate the difference between justice and injustice at the hands of the police.

Now to the role of the citizen who believes in friendly police and who is devoted to the proposition that liberty and justice are inseparable. Is there a part for each of us to play if we seek the good society? Indeed, there is! Note the phrasing of a previous sentence: "When the police serve as an agency of justice, we should in all good conscience regard the agency as a friend." We *should,* but we *don't.* And this lack of self-discipline may account, as much as any other reason, for the loss of liberty and justice, for runaway police.

It occurs to me that the required discipline may be more unknown than carelessly glossed over. John Philpot Curran said:

> The condition upon which God hath given liberty to man is eternal vigilance; which condition if he break, servitude is at once the consequence of his crime, and the punishment of his guilt.

This oft-repeated axiom is, in my view, the missing discipline. True, the words are well known; it's the meaning that's not known or even suspected. The axiom sounds good, but actually, what does one do to be forever vigilant? How exercise this discipline?

Yes, we rail against injustice but we do not know how to hail justice—or so I believe. Merely take note of the fact that when and if a policeman does something that's just—consistent with liberty—we do no more than regard it as the what-ought-to-be and let it go at that. Not vigilance at all; merely static acquiescence. In favor of justice, yes; vigilant standard-bearers, rarely, if ever.

This raises the final question: How does one become a vigilant standard-bearer? Would that it were as simple as a pat on the back to those police who do what's right and just! And even this would be simple, for there are ever so many who so conduct themselves but whose actions we never hear about. Mere praise does not suffice. All well and dandy, but there's nothing vigilant about that.

What then? The police agencies might soon rise to their principled role were their millions of members to stand ramrod straight. But this for certain, *they will never so behave short of some exemplars among the citizenry.*

Eternal vigilance is nothing less than exemplarity of the highest order on your part and mine—day in and day out, now and forever. A society gets the policemen it deserves; for the police agencies are no more than a reflection of you and me. We aid and abet what's good and just on the part of the police by being good ourselves—by nothing less than personal standard-setting performances.

17

WHAT WE CAN LEARN FROM A COMMUNIST

Hideous dreams are exaggerations of the sins of the day.

—EMERSON

Earl Browder was for years head of the Communist Party in the U.S.A. In a 1950 pamphlet, *Keynes, Foster and Marx: State Capitalism and Progress,* Browder listed 22 specific examples of the development of socialism in the United States:

1. government deficit financing
2. manipulation of bank reserve requirements
3. insurance of bank deposits
4. guarantee of mortgages
5. control of bank credits
6. tinkering with the currency system
7. regulation of installment buying
8. price controls
9. price supports for farm products.
10. agricultural credits
11. R.F.C. loans to business corporations

12. social security systems for workers
13. various benefits for veterans
14. government housing
15. public works to provide employment
16. many projects for the conservation of natural resources
17. juggling of the tax structure
18. new tariff regulations
19. government-organized foreign loans
20. the Employment Act
21. the President's Economic Committee
22. last, but by no means least, stimulated war armaments production on a large scale.

Concerning these 22 items, Mr. Browder wrote: "They have the single feature in common that . . . they express *the growth of state capitalism* . . . an essential feature of the confirmation of the Marxist theory. . . . It represents the maturing of the objective (material) prerequisites for socialism, the basic factor which makes socialism inevitable. . . ."

One can hardly deny that the trend summarized above takes us headlong into socialism. And there is a valuable lesson for all of us in Browder's further assertion: "State capitalism leaped forward to a new high point in America in the decade 1939-1949. . . . State capitalism, in substance if not in formal aspects, had progressed farther in America than in Great Britain under the Labor Government, despite its nationalization of certain industries, which is a formal stage not yet reached in America; the actual, substantial *concentration of the guiding reins of national economy in governmental hands* is probably on a higher level in the U.S.A. (Italics mine)

Precisely, what did Browder reveal here? What is the lesson for students of liberty? Unfortunately, most of us never suspect the advance of state capitalism until we see the means of production *formally* nationalized—such as mail delivery in all nations, the railroads and airlines in most nations, the telephones and banks in many, the steel mills in some, and so on. Browder correctly suggested that *formal* nationalization is, indeed, but a technicality, that the growth of state capitalism is to be measured by the "concentration of the guiding reins of national economy in governmental hands." Browder saw that the substance of communism is more important than the form. That's one lesson we should learn from a skilled devotee of communism.

So far as the nationalization of industry, commerce, finance, and agriculture is concerned, we in the U.S.A. have had but one formalization in the last 120 years: mail delivery.[1] Yet, in the 26 years since 1949, the end of the decade Browder so cogently assessed, the "concentration of the guiding reins of national economy in governmental hands" has increased enormously. Another lesson, unless we insist on rejecting a truth simply because it was uttered by a communist, is crystal clear: we are plunging into state capitalism—the communist ideal—without knowing what we are doing!

Perhaps some of the confusion about communism stems from the formal definition of it as the state ownership of the means or tools of production—property—with little if any real understanding of the significance of property rights and uses. As to rights, does a person have a right to the fruits (property) of his own labor? The student of liberty answers in the affirmative; the communist answers in the negative, as-

[1]There have been a few exceptions: the railroads on several occasions, and some nationalization of the power and light industry.

serting that all property shall be held in common, that is, by the state. State capitalism, they call it.

As to use, the tools of production (property) are in scarce supply. How are they to be allocated? Who is to get how much of what? The student of liberty contends that allocation should be left to willing exchange in a free market; the communist insists that allocation of scarce resources shall be by a centralized political control.

Property—access to valuable resources—is simply a tool to help satisfy human desires. As long as the ownership and use of property is determined and guided by the market forces of open competition, everyone has access to these valuable resources in proportion to his own productive effort. Private ownership means personal control over the tools of production and, thus, personal control over one's life. But when government owns and controls the property and thereby denies the functioning of the market, then government controls lives. Communism is, in fact, people control, as is every intervention into the market by the state.

All one needs to understand is that private ownership disappears as private control is lost. There is no such thing as ownership without control. One may have a deed to his property; but if he has no say-so as to its disposition, the piece of paper is utterly meaningless.[2] Thus, when there is a "concentration of the guiding reins of national economy in

[2]The sole distinction between the Russian version of socialism (called communism) and the once-upon-a-time Italian version of socialism (called fascism) is that in Russia the government holds title to all tools of production, except a few private plots, and in Italy the meaningless titles were retained by those who once were owners. The U.S.A., by not going through the formalities of nationalization, that is, by letting owners retain titles as control is taken over by the government, is following the Italian pattern. But it is only the difference between tweedle-dee and tweedle-dum.

governmental hands," state capitalism displaces private capitalism. Control *is* ownership!

Why do we so generally and stubbornly refuse to heed the lessons here set forth? Try another question, and the answer may reveal itself: *Just what, pray tell, do we think communism is?*

There will be little certainty among most of us as to what communism is except some hated, ideological ogre, originating with a clique of foreign conspirators. As to what it is, the answers will, for the most part, be at the definitive level of, "It's something awful." And, whatever communism is, we Americans, by and large, have no doubt whatsoever that it is clearly un-American! By a vague definition designed to skirt self-blame, it is, perforce, a way of life we do not indulge in or have any part of. It is from such confusions in definition that communism spreads so rapidly in America.

Not a one of us, who does any thinking at all, will question the fact that collectivized farming, as practiced in Russia, is communistic to the core. Agreed, coercive collectivization and communization are interchangeable terms. Everyone knows that! Obviously, collectivized farming is the perfect example of communism in the economic realm. But here's the rub: How many of us will discern communism in any of the 22 items listed by Earl Browder? Very few! Yet, communism, as Browder pointed out, is the essence of every last one of them.

Pick one at random—1 to 22—guaranteed mortgages is as good as any to make the point. What! Are we to call guaranteed mortgages communistic? An accepted American practice for fifty-five years! Why, people will think we're out of our minds. But they will be wrong for, if we will use our minds, we can see through that hocus-pocus just as clearly as did Browder. The revealing and key word is "guaranteed." Guaranteed by whom—that is, who is the guarantor? The answer comes clear and clean: the government. The government has nothing of its own, so what is the collateral which leads us to believe that the guarantee is valid? Nothing except the government's taxing power. Thus, the "guarantee" consists of *coercively collectivized collateral,* differing not at all in principle from collectivized farming as practiced in Russia. Any of the other 21 items listed by Browder can as easily be analyzed and understood as this one.

If we reject communism—which I do—then we must understand and practice its alternative: the common consent, willing exchange way of life, the right to the fruits of one's own labor being implicit in such a market economy. Complete the arrangement by limiting the activities of the police force to keeping the peace and, thus, be done with communism in America.

Reflect on how happy Earl Browder would be today—his dream coming nearer to reality during each of the 25 years since his contribution to our learning. And how happy *we* should be! With his accurate removal of the camouflage, we can make his ugly dream so far from realization that he, if alive, would be an unhappy communist. The love of liberty and the abhorrence of communism is a source of happiness to me—and doubtless to you!

18

FROM WHOM SEEK PRAISE?

It is easier to find a score of men wise enough to discover the truth, than to find one intrepid enough, in the face of opposition, to stand up for it.

—A. A. HODGE

There are ever so many men and women wise enough to discover bits of truth, but few indeed are those intrepid enough—in the face of opposition—to stand up for it. How shall we account for such intellectual timidity? Part of the answer is surely to be sought in a misguided interpretation of the democratic ethos, in the notion that truth is a matter of consensus. For if that be the test of truth, then the person who stands—alone if need be—for his convictions is wrong! When "truth" is redefined as majority opinion, then the seeker after "truth" is actually bent on winning a popularity contest!

Most of us know better; things are what they are, regardless of what a majority says they are. Any stalwart embraces his convictions because he believes them to be true, no matter what the consensus. Our ancestors would have phrased it somewhat differently: "seek not your praise before men, but before God"—let Righteousness be the goal. Persons who understand and keep this distinction in mind will not be deterred by opposition; they will stand by their beliefs, whatever the changing winds of opinion. If we will look at it this way, perhaps we can understand why some few among us are intrepid enough to stand up for the bits of truth that may grace their awareness, perception, consciousness.

Reflect on what happens when praise is sought from man—any man. No two persons have identical intellectual, politico-economic, moral, and spiritual views. And unless one be stagnated—not growing—he does not himself have the same ideas from one day to the next. So, when we seek praise from man, we are trying to imitate or be guided by a very unstable model—a fallible human being whose ideas are forever moving this way and that; this instability is true even of "leaders" who are celebrated or famous, great or adored. If a person stakes his all on any man's approval, and fails to attain it, chances are he will not be and cannot be intrepid enough to withstand the opposition. Will not his opposition be those he holds up as models and imitates? No one is intrepid enough to stand up to that confusion.

Seeking praise from one man, regardless of who he might be, is error of the first order. The debilitating consequence is timid souls rather than intrepid ones, and the fear of opposition rather than the welcome of open competition. Move now to those who seek praise not from a man but from men, a majority, let us say. This is what guides most politicians.

Stand in opposition to the consensus? Rarely! This largely accounts for our trek down the road to serfdom.

Do we not observe this same procedure in the "teachings" of ever so many college and university professors? They take great care not to depart too far from the notions that compose the academic consensus. When Keynesianism is the mode, as now, they go along with Keynes. The primary aim is approval by one's contemporaries; truth is secondary. Thus is righteousness spurned by countless thousands of "teachers" who curry favor—seek praise.

Think of the persons in your own orbit who seek praise from men rather than standing foursquare for Righteousness—a moral position grounded on reason and supported by evidence. One observes this catering to majority-opinion in all walks of life and in all professions; in clergymen who no more seek Righteousness (praise before God) than do politicians, or teachers, or labor officials, or businessmen, or any other kind of man.

To speak of "praise" before God, as the Bible has it, may, by reason of the evolution of this word from Aramaic to Greek, Latin, French, and English, evoke a meaning not originally intended. According to the *Oxford Dictionary* the word "praise" was "not known till after 1400, and not common till after 1500."

True, we give praise to and receive praise from men, but what was intended by the original usage of the word? According to the English philosopher, Hobbes (1588-1679): "The forms of speech whereby men signifie their opinion of Goodnesse of any thing, is Praise." The few who do not seek praise from either man or God manifest their high "opinion of Goodnesse" by praising God, Truth, Righteousness. The distinction between the many and the few is clear: the few do not *seek* praise from anything or anybody; they *give* praise!

You and I give praise to others—past and present—and some of our contemporaries occasionally give praise to us. All well and good! But take note of how spontaneously we are turned off when others, in effect, beg for our praise. Such *seeking* of praise for one's self puts an end to the *giving* of praise. Why? Asking for praise is a perversion of self-esteem. Who cares to puff up an already bloated ego by praising it?

As to the other side of this behavioral coin, George Washington gave of his wisdom:

> If to please the people, we offer what we ourselves disapprove, how can we afterward defend our work? Let us raise a standard to which the wise and honest can repair. The event is in the hand of God.

The "standard to which the wise and honest can repair" is Righteousness, and contains not an iota of opposition. To the contrary, Righteousness affords an infinite potential and the sole obstruction is one's own inadequacy—which he alone may expect to overcome.

By *giving praise* to Righteousness, day in and day out, we keep constantly in mind the "standard to which the wise and honest can repair," thus making it less difficult to overcome our own inadequacy. By so doing, fears are replaced by aspirations and hopes. And the seekers of praise are replaced by the givers thereof. Thus, may we reverse our present course which leads to serfdom and turn again toward freedom!

19

RISING TO MORAL HEIGHTS

If I knew the world would come to pieces tomorrow, I would still plant my apple tree.

—UNKNOWN

My dictionary tells me that a *Saying* "is a simple, direct term for any pithy expression of wisdom or truth." The above is assuredly a "saying" for it is pithy, it is wise, it is true —or so it seems to me. For I firmly believe that anyone who looks upon his mortal moment in this manner has intelligently comprehended his role in this world: rising to moral heights!

When I speak of moral heights I refer to the highest possible state of righteousness! It is to understand and adhere to the several virtues. It includes a humility so advanced that there isn't even the desire to run the lives of others; and an integrity so well developed that word and deed are accurate reflections of the truth as one sees it. And certainly the Golden Rule: never doing to others that which would be objectionable if done to you.

Immanuel Kant had a yardstick for measuring moral heights, one that all of us might well adopt: "In every case I must so act that I can at the same time will that the maxim behind my act should become a universal law." In a word, behave in a manner that would be agreeable to you were everyone else to so behave. Here we have a rational morality. On this point, C. S. Lewis observed:

> I am very doubtful whether history shows us one example of a man who, having stepped outside *rational morality* and attained power, has used that power benevolently.

The American statesman, Charles Sumner, gave wise support to this thought:

> The true grandeur of humanity is in moral elevation, sustained, enlightened and decorated by the intellect of man.

In any event, the above roughly defines what I mean by "moral heights" and suggests the importance thereof.

If I knew the world would come to pieces tomorrow! No one, of course, knows what is going to happen from minute to minute, let alone from day to day, or on any tomorrow.

Come what may, for better or worse, the world on the upswing or going to pot—the future is beyond the range of any person's say-so. What then? The individual wise enough to seek moral heights knows that he is but an infinitesimal part of mankind; that the world of humanity is not his to govern or control; that each is a creature, under a Creator, each responsible for his own actions and their consequences.

Potentially, he can exercise a determining influence over his own tomorrow and that's as much as any individual can do. In brief, this means that regardless of what happens, "I would still plant my apple tree."

I would still plant my apple tree! How is this beautiful

imagery to be interpreted? Note that it's *my* planting—not yours or anyone else's. Why this emphasis on the self? That only I can do my planting is a rarely recognized truth; persons in countless numbers are fruitlessly trying to do your plantings and mine—transplanting, we might call it.

And why an apple tree? Three reasons: (1) it reaches for the heavens, that is, for heights; (2) its roots go deep; and (3) it bears fruit!

Observe that the leaves of an apple tree reach for the Sun, that is, they draw energy from above—the photosynthetic process. Man, likewise, may reach for moral heights, forever exploring unknown truths, those not yet of this world.

The roots? They reach into the fertility of mother earth and draw water and nourishment from the soil and store food. Comparable human action is man reaching for those bits of wisdom that are of this world, many of which may be found if diligently sought.

Both the leaves and the roots draw nutriment, neither of which can be cut off from the other, except in a period of dormancy, without the tree's decay. The two must perform as one or the tree is done, and will bear no apples. Comparable is man reaching for the unknown and the known—for established wisdom and for new insights. Both explorations are necessary if the individual is to bear fruit and attain moral heights.

Finally, why dwell on this imagery? Simply to remind myself of the way I should order my own life! Regardless of what happens to my little world, I must still plant my apple tree—reach for moral heights. My personal world is the only one I have been commissioned to oversee, popular opinions to the contrary notwithstanding.

Is fulfilling such a minor commission important? Indeed so! There is no assignment in the life of man that requires more devoted attention than this. Why this claim? The freedom way of life—individual liberty which allows each to become his creative and divinely ordained self—is the very essence of *rational morality*. Apart from this, I am condemned to live in a world totalitarian rather than free, which of course, lessens the healthy prospects for earthly pilgrimage. Thus, self-interest dictates that I reach for moral heights.

But what about the little world of my neighbor who lives here, there, and everywhere? How does the rational morality of any one of us bear on his situation? As much as is within your or my power! In this realm, exemplarity is the only tool any one of us possesses. To repeat, example is more caught than taught. If it be good enough—sufficiently magnetic—one or more will doubtless emulate. So, what can I do for others? I can plant and tend my apple tree.

20
IDEAS ARE REAL

The idea of liberty must grow weak in the hearts of men before it can be killed at the hands of tyrants.

According to Richard Weaver, *Ideas Have Consequences.*[1] Indeed they do! We act out our beliefs. All human action stems from ideas, be they good, bad, or indifferent. Ideas direct the course of life toward its fulfillment or its waste—from an economic point of view, toward plenitude or poverty. Ideas are as real as life itself, and they exist in infinite variety.

Reflect on the familiar phrase, "Beauty is in the eye of the beholder." There are those who behold no beauty in anything, any time, anywhere; they grub through a gray existence. On the other hand are those rare souls who behold beauty everywhere—on earth and in the heavens—in atoms and galaxies, snowflakes and raindrops, blades of grass and towering hemlocks, the rising and setting sun, clouds and lightning and

[1]*Ideas Have Consequences* by Richard M. Weaver (Chicago: The University of Chicago Press, 1948)

thunder. Also, they behold beauty in such exemplary works of man as paintings, musical compositions, cookery, or countless other manifestations of excellence. Yet, even these rare souls behold but an infinitesimal fraction of the true and beautiful. The beholder's eye is finite and, at best, can no more than catch a glimpse of the infinite wonders of Creation.

While beauty is in the *eye of the beholder,* ideas are in the *heart or mind of the perceiver.* Otherwise, beholding and perceiving appear to be comparable in many ways. For there are those who go through their mortal moment addicted more to imitation than graced with perceptive abilities. However, a few rare souls perceive ideas on as vast a scale as some others behold beauty. Gifted or acquired? Each person is unique in this respect, as in all others!

True, much of what we perceive is what others have already noted and brought to our attention. But what about the previous perceivers? What was their source? To me, the fountainhead is shrouded in mystery, as is the source of all that is beautiful. I, for instance, perceive from Emerson that which he perceived before me:

> We lie in the lap of *immense intelligence* which makes us receivers [perceivers] of its truth and organs of its activity. When we discern justice, when we discern truth, we do nothing of ourselves, but allow a passage of its beams.

In a word, no person may be said to originate an idea any more than you or I originate beauty in its infinite variations. The most that can be said of anyone is that he was the original perceiver—identification impossible. The first perceiver of any idea can no more be identified than the first individual to behold the beauty of the aurora borealis!

The idea of liberty must grow weak in the hearts of men. . . . What is that idea? Find the answer to the question: What is truth? And this is no easier than finding the answer to: What is Infinite Consciousness? My definition: Truth is that which one's highest conscience dictates as right. This may not in fact be Truth but it is the closest you or I or anyone else can come to Truth. Likewise, the idea of liberty has an infinity of origins, as does that of beauty.

At the human level of perception, we have only those bits of Truth come upon by the wise. Here follows a few I have perceived, but only after reading the works of Edmund Burke who perceived them ahead of me—two centuries beforehand! Take note of the varying ideas which, according to Burke, must be perceived and adhered to lest liberty grow weak in the hearts and minds of men.

- Men are qualified for civil liberty in exact proportion to their disposition to put chains upon their own appetites;
- in proportion as their love of justice is above their rapacity;
- in proportion as their soundness and sobriety of understanding is above their vanity and presumption;
- in proportion as they are more disposed to listen to the counsels of the wise and good, in preference to the flattery of knaves.
- Society cannot exist unless a controlling power upon the will and appetite is placed somewhere; and the less of it there is within, the more there must be of it without.
- It is ordained in the eternal constitution of things, that men of intemperate habits cannot be free. *Their passions forge their fetters.*

Is the idea of liberty growing weak in the hearts of men? Merely assess Burke's excellent guidelines. Were we to weigh mankind in general, the conclusion would be most discouraging; liberty is losing. But we know the idea of liberty is on the upgrade in the hearts of numerous individuals. So, the answer hangs in the balance.

Before it can be killed at the hands of tyrants. Who are the tyrants? Quintus Ennius, a Latin poet of 23 centuries ago, perceived the answer, "Men who know not their own path, yet point the way for others." Being neither a Roman nor a poet, I would phrase it thus: Men who have stagnated, who are so ignorant that they know not how little they know, yet coercively force others to labor on collective farms as in Russia, or forbid free production and exchange and competition as in the U.S.A. They kill not only liberty but the idea of liberty. These stagnated "beings" are our fetters which those of "intemperate habits" forge.

From all of the above it is easy to despair, as so many do, of spreading the idea of liberty to the point where it is again strong in the hearts and minds of men. But not so! Wrote one of the wisest men, Albert Schweitzer, "Example is not the *main* thing in influencing others. It is the *only* thing." Ideas, while real, can no more be taught than can beauty. *The idea of liberty can only be caught!* From whom? Exemplars!

Turning again to Burke's guidelines, let us consider whether it is possible for you or me to become exemplars.

- Can we put chains upon our appetites? If capable of overcoming our weaknesses, yes!
- What about the love of justice? This is out of the question for those who have stagnated but a natural trait

for anyone who is growing in awareness, perception, consciousness.

- Soundness and sobriety of understanding? This intellectual achievement ascends as the love of justice intensifies. The two are wedded!
- Listen to the counsels of the wise and good rather than to the flattery of knaves? There is no easier way to personal upgrading. It is nothing more than to take advantage of those who have perceived beforehand—a free service to enlightened self-interest.
- A controlling power upon will and appetite? We despise tyrants. To keep them from controlling us, nothing more is required than control within—self-control. To be without such self-control is to be a human nobody.
- Intemperate habits? Society-wise, the intemperate habits that make freedom impossible are born of know-it-all-ness, the little-god syndrome, be-like-me-ness—each a would-be dictocrat. "You fool" and countless other epithets—oral, written, and silent—are its earmarks. The cure lies in three easy steps: (1) a recognition of how infinitesimal is one's wisdom, (2) call not the sinner a fool, only the sin, and (3) heartily approve the freedom of everyone to act creatively as he chooses. Emulate the Lord rather than lording it over others!

Were the idea and practice of liberty a numbers problem, no chance! However, every advance in human history has been led by an infinitesimal minority—a few exemplars. Reflect upon the fact that West Germany, a devastated country following World War II, was turned into freedom and prosperity by three exemplars, the greatest demonstration of how freedom works its wonders in the Twentieth Century.[2]

---

[2]See "Right Now!", Chapter 26.

Three! There are tens of thousands in the U.S.A. today who favor the idea and practice of liberty. The improved practice depends upon the improved perception of the idea, for ideas are indeed real and have consequences. The results come from the examples we set. To the extent that you improve, to that extent will I be helped and vice versa. The formula is that simple and easy. Let us try to out-distance one another in our understanding and improvement. Have fun in this greatest contest in life and the idea of liberty will not—cannot—be killed at the hands of tyrants. *We will win!*

21

ON GIVING AND RECEIVING

It is more blessed to give than to receive.

—ACTS XX:35

Before expressing my unorthodox views on giving and receiving, let me set the stage for its economic significance by commenting on its person-to-person relationship. But first, why unorthodox? Theologians, by and large, have thought of this biblical maxim only in an alms-giving sense, whereas, in my view, it has an additional meaning. That an additional meaning was intended is indicated by the fact that the same Bible that declares, "It is more blessed to give than to receive," also carries the admonition that "He who does not work shall not eat." (Thess. III:10.)

In the mind's eye, protrude a pipe from the dry side of Hoover Dam to Lake Mead. The pipe is capped on the dry side so no water will flow out and, by the same token, none will flow in. Now remove the cap. Water will flow out and an equal amount will flow in; the giving off is the *precedent* to the inflow.

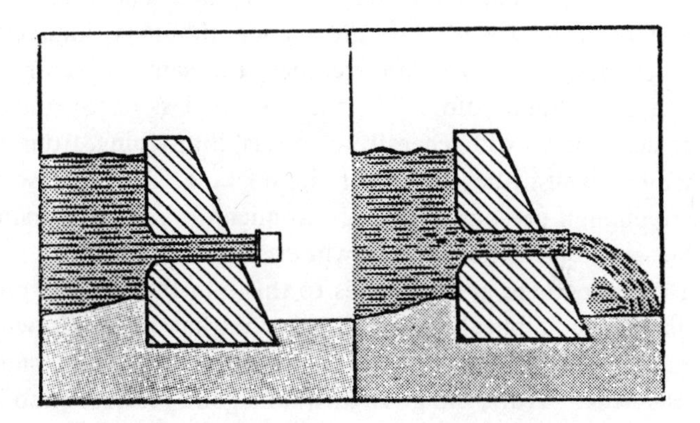

By the action of giving off, the potential energy of Lake Mead is converted into moving, power-giving, kinetic energy. This is the nature of hydraulic energy. Here the analogy ends for the giving off does not increase the amount of water in Lake Mead.

In the case of intellectual energy, the greater the outflow the more the inflow. Thus, one of the reasons it is "more blessed to give than to receive" is that the giving off of good ideas and thoughts—enlightenments—is the *precedent* to the reception of new ones, that is, a conversion of potential to realized aptitudes. The more one shares these blessings with others, the more does he receive, the more is he blest.

The experiences of numerous persons attest to the fact that the more they share ideas with others, the more ideas they receive and the higher grade are the ideas. This is easy to explain. When one shares, whether in discoursing, lecturing, or writing, he puts his best foot forward. And what can be more upgrading than everlastingly striving to do one's best!

When one believes the best of every man and gives evidence of it, and when one gives good thoughts, kindness, respect, affection, love, one receives the same in return—perhaps "a thousandfold"! It is a more or less unrecognized fact that thieves will generally steal less, if anything, from individuals well disposed, and it should be evident that were there enough persons of this moral mien, thievery and many other evils of mankind would wither away.

However, there are two sides to this unorthodox interpretation of our biblical maxim, a side that has not to do with blessings but, if I may descend to the vernacular, with "pains in the neck." Truly, the giver of what's good receives good in return. But, just as truly, the giver of what's bad receives bad in return. In a word, the giver—you or me or anyone—pretty much makes his own little world by the kind of a person he makes of himself.

He who hates is hated in return, usually receiving more hate than he gives. And the same can be said for disdain, disrespect, ill will. Defamers are in turn defamed. The know-it-all breeds the know-it-alls who increasingly surround him. Those of the dictocratic blight spawn political dictatorship. Anger? Wrote Alexander Pope, *"To be angry is to revenge the faults of others on ourselves."* Reflect on the faults in all of us. Anger causes the faults inherent in others to roost in the angry ones. The giving of anger assures a return in kind from those at whom it is directed. Whoever observed affection or esteem as a response to a fit of anger! Virtues are not cultivated but are deadened by this vice—in the giver and receiver alike.

Yes, on a person-to-person basis, one pretty much makes his own little world. He receives what he gives, be it good or bad and, thus, to a marked extent is the master of his personal domain. But when it comes to the world at large—the enormous societal domain—he is no longer master. Each of us is but a human drop in a vast sea of humanity. The politico-economic situation does not come under the governance of you or me or any individual. But be it noted that thieves are found in the best of these units, just as men of great virtues are observed in the worst of them. Yet, I prefer not only for myself but for others a civilized rather than a barbaric environment. Given such a preference, what can you or I do about it? That's the question.

If a civilized society be our preference, the utmost anyone can do to achieve it is through his personal domain. This, I feel certain, is the way it should be. To whom should we assign a control over the creative lives of citizens greater than the attractive power implicit in his own excellence? Not to anyone nor to any combination of persons, be the one a self-acclaimed god or the combination a "democratic" congress!

Those of us who seek to foster a civilized society are limited to what we can achieve by personal exemplarity. Beyond this we cannot go, nor is there need that we should. The internationally known Viennese psychiatrist, Dr. Viktor E. Frankl, explains why:

> As for environment, we know that it does not make man, that everything depends on what man makes of it, on his attitude toward it.[1]

---

[1]*See The Doctor & the Soul* by Viktor E. Frankl, M.D., Ph.D. (New York: Vintage Books, 1973), p. xxix.

In other words, to the extent that we as individuals are pure in thought and deed, to that extent is the sea of humanity—the environment—in a state of purity. With respect to social improvement, we need only give what is good and refrain from giving what is bad, precisely as in person-to-person relationships. There follow a few samplings of what is meant by this.

Let me begin with another ancient axiom, this one from the Hindu bible, *The Bhagavadgita:*

> Sin is . . . [that] ignorance . . . which seeks its own gain at the expense of others.[2]

Sin and ignorance are here equated, and why not! The message? To gain at the expense of others is not only an ignorant way of life but it is sinful. To practice this sin is to invite reprisal in kind—doubtless multiplied!

Common thievery is looked upon by nearly everyone as an ignorant way of life. It is self-evident that all would perish were all thieves. Also seen clearly is the ignorance of tribes invading their neighbors and taking home the loot. But only a very few see anything ignorant in feathering their own nests at the expense of others if it's done on the authority of majority vote, as in the U.S.A. today on an enormous scale. State welfarism is no less an ignorant way of life than are the discredited ways of thieves or marauding tribes.

Very well! What can we do about such ignorance or sin? Here is the sequence as I see it:

1. To understand and everlastingly practice their opposites: virtue and intelligence.

---

[2]From *The Bhagavadgita;* translated by S. Radhakrishnan (New York: Harper & Bros., 1948), p. 224.

2. To recognize that the sole virtuous way to feather any nest is with the fruits of one's own labor, not with that of others.
3. Let each give of this intelligence as in person-to-person relationships and all will receive more; thievery in its various forms will give way to freedom, self-responsibility, and an improved welfare for all.

Next, how should a good economist appraise the advantages of freedom and self-responsibility? Reflect on these two points, admittedly oversimplified:

1. Learn to recognize and to beware of freedom's opposite: coercive actions to attain special privileges. In this category are tariffs and all restraints to trade, including many actions of labor unions that rely on government sanction or intervention. The list is nigh endless.
2. Aspire to an awareness of how the free market works its wonders and why.[3] Embrace that absolute principle: freedom in transactions.[4] In a word, understand and be able to explain why free and unfettered exchange between individuals—local, national, and international—is the way to an increasing abundance for all and, further, the way to peace on earth and good will toward men!

A final thought on giving and receiving, this having to do with attitudes. Again, opposites: faith and fear.

To be remembered above all else is that each of us has only

[3]For my best explanation, see *Castles in the Air* (Irvington, N.Y.: The Foundation for Economic Education, Inc., 1975), pp. 7-21.

[4]See *Economic Sophisms* by Frederic Bastiat (Irvington, N.Y.: The Foundation for Economic Education, Inc., 1964), pp. 96-97.

his own little world to manage and to perfect. If this is done to the very best of one's ability, he may trust with confidence in the overall outcome.

Finally, let our efforts be joyful—have fun! The perfection of self—growth in awareness, perception, consciousness—should be life's most enjoyable experience. Exuberance—along with variety—is part of the spice of life.

22
LOOKING FOR THE MAGIC KEY

Let us not look back in anger, nor forward in fear, but around in awareness.

—**JAMES THURBER**

"Oh, that the world might be turned around to suit my fancy; what a boon to mankind that would be!" This is rather a common notion, slightly entertained if not openly pronounced, on both sides of the ideological fence. Marx, Keynes, and their kind, past and present, yes. But among the devotees of freedom also are to be found glaring examples, now more than ever—doubtless because events are going so contrary to our views.

Here is a confession: I *have been* thus afflicted. Every time I noted a flip-flop from a socialistic to a freedom position, I would inquire as to the cause—searching always for the magic key. Once I had found it, so I presumed, then I alone could turn the world around. Here are a few of my observations in that regard.

One of the best workers in freedom's vineyard in the country today is an individual I first met in 1946. He confessed to me that, when he graduated from college, he was a socialist. So I asked him, "What turned you around?" He replied, "It was that chapter in Hayek's *Road to Serfdom* entitled 'Why The Worst Get On Top.'" Tens of thousands of Hayek's book have been sold. How many, in reading that interesting and enlightening chapter, were transformed in philosophy? I have never heard of another. No magic key there! Nonetheless, I kept right on looking for it.

A brilliant young man, a graduate student at the University of Chicago and a first-rate devotee of freedom, remarked to me, "When I came out of the Bronx High School of Science, I was a socialist."

"How come? What caused the change?"

"It was George Reisman."

"Yes, we know George, but what did he say or do?"

"Well, he was our guest for dinner and I was showing him our new refrigerator. Then George asked, 'Ron, how would you allocate refrigerators were it not for the market's pricing system?'" It was the market's allocation of scarce resources concept that turned me around."

I have searched in vain for another case where that bit of insight reversed anyone's ideological position. So I conclude that it isn't the magic key, either.

One more. A long-time friend of mine, a splendid thinker and writer—Verna Hall—drove from San Francisco to a place near Santa Cruz where we were conducting a FEE Seminar. She had one purpose only, namely, to introduce me to her friend, Rosalie Slater. Said Verna, "Rosalie has been doing graduate work at Stanford University preparing to become an administrator in the government school system; but lately has had a change of heart and wishes to ask you some questions." Verna returned to San Francisco, Rosalie to luncheon with me.

My first question, "Tell me, Miss Slater, how long have you been interested in this philosophy?" Her answer I had never heard before—or since: "Mr. Read, I have now been liberated for six months." Remarkable! I didn't ask Miss Slater what caused her "liberation" but, later, still looking for the magic key, I phoned Verna and inquired as to the cause. Her response: "Rosalie and I have been close friends for years. One evening we were philosophizing—not arguing—and I made the point that when one turns the responsibility for self over to another or lets government take it away, to the extent of the removal, to that extent the removal of the very essence of one's being. That's the idea that liberated Rosalie." Thus runs the story of another splendid worker in freedom's vineyard.

Did anyone ever hear of any other individual liberated by that bit of profound wisdom? I haven't! Anyway, these and many other experiences over the years have liberated me from such fruitless looking. *There isn't any magic key.*

What then? Is there no formula for assisting in the liberation of others? Of course there is: *see how many keys each of us can get on his own ring!* According to the law of probability, there is a greater chance that some one key among a thousand will unlock that door—liberate another—than will any single key. In a word, concentrate on the expansion of one's own repertoire.

James Thurber clearly grasped this important point in methodology:

Don't look back in anger at what's gone on. That makes opponents, not friends for freedom. Also, it is a cause of psychosomatic illness.

Don't fear that which lies ahead. First, no one knows; there isn't an accurate crystal ball reader in the population! Second, it's faith—believing—that enhances the chances of winning.

Rather, look to one's own awareness. Herein lies all the hope for the restoration of the free society! And as I see it, that's precisely the way it should be—the way it is.

It is easy to see why looking to one's own awareness is the correct tactic. Merely bear in mind that no one can insinuate an idea into the consciousness of another. Each individual is in charge of his own doors of perception. And anyone bent on learning looks only to those who, in his or her judgment, have light to shed. Excellence is the attracting force, be it golf, cooking, liberty, or whatever.

Assuming a person wishes enlightenment in free market, private ownership, limited government ideas and ideals—liberty—to whom is he attracted? To angry, fearful characters of the broken record variety? Rarely, and not for long! By and large, they are avoided by thoughtful seekers, *the only ones who matter.* To whom then? To those who have an enlarged repertoire—the more keys on their ring, the greater the magnetism! For confirmation, reflect on personal experiences.

My liberation from fruitless methods has, over the past forty-five years, been achieved the hard way. Select any of the methods, now so much on the rampage—from name-calling to "selling the masses"—I've tried them all! But when found wanting—utterly fruitless or downright harmful—I have abandoned them—every one! With the futile schemes tossed overboard, what remains? It is the *law of attraction,* applying no less to individual relationships than to atoms, solar systems, or galaxies. From a noted astronomer:

> All of the phenomena of astronomy, which had baffled the acutest minds since the dawn of history, the movement of the heavens, of the sun and the moon, the very complex movement of the planets, suddenly tumble together and become intelligible in terms of the one staggering assumption, the mysterious *"attractive force."* And not only the movements of the heavenly bodies, far more than that, the movements of earthly bodies, too, are seen to be subject to the same mathematically definable law, instead of being, as they were for all previous philosophers, mere unpredictable happen-so's.[1]

In my judgment, one hasn't a prayer of being an effective worker in freedom's vineyard except as he grasps and adheres strictly to the law of attraction—that magnetism founded exclusively on the pursuit of excellence. Doubtless, many freedom devotees are influenced to employ wrong methods because of the success of such methods in destroying a free society. But creating a free society is a different matter and so must the methods be different. The methods that work in destroying are destructive when used in creating. Now for a few reflections.

So far as change for the better is concerned, it has its beginning with self-change. Observed William Hazlitt: "Consider how hard it is to change yourself, and you will understand what little chance you have to change others." An appreciation of this difficulty is step number one for anyone.

[1]*Science Is A Sacred Cow* by Anthony Standen (New York: E. P. Dutton and Company, Inc., 1950), pp. 63-64.

Do I inspire a change for the better in another? Answer that correctly and one has his measure of influence for the good as related to humanity.

Let one's ambition be to reflect, not effect. The reverse is a perversion of cause and effect, of means and ends.

"Nearly everyone seems anxious to serve in an advisory capacity." The cure for this malady? Await the seeking of counsel! But what if no one seeks? It's a signal: there's homework to do!

In the creative or improvement realm, there are no reformers: there are those who attract, as distinguished from would-be reformers who repel.

Has anyone ever remembered falling asleep? I doubt it! This may account for an unawareness of the intellectual and spiritual slumber, a distressing feature of our time. We do, however, remember coming awake—perhaps a cue for some helpful self-assessment.

Now to the positive. Margaret Slattery, a British churchwoman, entitled a lecture, THEY THOUGHT, THEY DID—AND SO THEY BECAME. There's enough wisdom in these few words for all the correction we need.

Gerald Heard spoke of the three stages of growth: conduct, character, and consciousness. "First, we will to conduct ourselves a little better. Our improved conduct becomes habitual and shapes our character, *and eventually there is a breakthrough into a higher level of consciousness."* Simple? Yes! Difficult? Of course! But this is what our problem is all about, and there are no short cuts.

Finally, there is a misunderstanding to be corrected. There are people who contend that an unequivocal stand for the free society is an attempt to turn the world around to suit *our* fancy.

Not so! It is, instead, an attempt to free human beings from all dictocrats, those who try to turn the world to their fancy. The freedom philosophy suggests that each individual be permitted to go his merry way—creatively, that is. The free man is allowed to try his own way—not to be turned my way or anyone else's!

23

BE-ATTITUDES

He who is cowardly will do right because it is safer *to do so. . .*

He who is overly ambitious will do right if it is to his advantage *to do so. . .*

He who is miserly will do right when he finds it cheaper *to do so. . .*

He who is average will do right because it is expected *of him. . .*

But blessed is he who does right because it is *right.*

Doing right just because it is right is as good a formula as exists for the salvation of one's soul; but my concern here is on the external importance of right action. Undeniably, the fate of each of us is somewhat determined by what goes on in the world outside. The fate of our nation or society has much more to do with your destiny and mine than is generally supposed. Yet, the world outside of us is governed by what goes on inside—in the heads—of individuals.

Suppose, for instance, that every freedom devotee in our country were a pessimist, certain that the way of life we cherish is doomed. Doom it would be, for it is evident that "fear tends to make fears come true."

Envision the opposite: Every freedom devotee an optimist, certain of winning. A victory it would be, for there is daily evidence that faith—believing—works miracles. The results of this frame of mind—intellectual ascension— are as certain as the results of fear—intellectual declension. Favoring optimism, as I do, is one thing; explaining it is more difficult, but very important. So let me try.

I would first call attention to the extent to which freedom is supported by those who do what's right for material motives—because it pays off in a more comfortable life. Without such backing, freedom's plight would be far worse than now.

Reflect on the millions too cowardly to confess that they are as socialistic or communistic as their thoughts and talk suggest. Instead of retreating behind the Iron Curtain, they stay where it's *safer* and partake of the fruits of private ownership and trade in the free market. Much that they do is right, but they *do* it more out of habit than conviction.

Reflect on those who are overly ambitious, not for purposes of self-improvement, but for glorification, fame, to be celebrated, their name "on the tip of every tongue." Yet, they will do right when it is to their *advantage* to do so. And ever so many times it is advantageous to hail "the American way of life" and utter other patriotisms that bring acclaim and fame.

Reflect on those who are miserly and will do right when it is *cheaper* to do so. Their frugality warrants no special applause, but the miserly generally do right as bargain hunters who reward and assure the success of efficient producers.

Reflect on those who are average and will do right because it is *expected* of them. Expected by whom? Those who do right because it is right! Thus, those who are "average" do an enormous amount of right, a great boon to freedom even though not guided by high principles and personal integrity.

Now to my point: Blessed is he who does right because it *is* right. Running away in fear is a common weakness. A quitter is distressed by everything that happens in his personal life regarded as unfavorable, be it criticism, disagreement, illness, a deserting friend, on and on to the end of his mortal moment. In a word: worrycrat!

But fretting about personal problems is only half of such a person's dilemma. This fainthearted individual is distressed—pessimistic—about everything that goes on in society that doesn't accord with his views of what-ought-to-be—a faulty attitude! True, much that is happening today is gravely at odds with what any freedom devotee regards as right and proper. However, this is no time to give up in despair. As Josiah Holland put it: "A time like this demands strong minds, great hearts, true faith, and ready hands."[1]

Finally, he who does right because it *is* right is psychologically, intellectually, morally, and spiritually attuned to reality. He is no more offended by criticism than elated by praise. Nor is he downcast by the errors of others, for he does not think of himself as the ONE who should order their lives.

---

[1]"The Day's Demand" by Josiah G. Holland (1819-1881). *Essays on Liberty,* Vol. VII, p. 9.

Whatever goes on in his personal life or in the world around him are facts to be taken into consideration by him as he acts and reacts. But fretting will not change such facts. He is, by reason of this high resolve, an optimist, for he is positive that he can do what's right because it *is* right.

24

THE SCHOOL OF MANKIND

Example is the school of mankind;
they learn at no other.

—BURKE

That scholarly and brilliant Britisher, Edmund Burke (1727-1797), assuredly used the term "mankind" as defined in his country's *Oxford Dictionary:* "Human beings in general." Thus, the reference was not to those few who think for themselves and explore the Unknown, the ones graced with insights and who experience intuitive flashes, the moral and intellectual giants, the oversouls, those like Confucius, Socrates, Epictetus, Augustine, Maimonides, Adam Smith and thousands of others. Not included in Burke's dictum were those who rank high in setting examples—the exemplars! Rather, his reference was to the general run of us who learn, if at all, by the example of our superiors.

For the past forty years I have studied the few—those stalwarts past and present—and observed how their exemplarity has helped me to shape my life. They teach by the high example they set, and we learn by our efforts to do likewise. To the extent that we learn the lessons their examples teach, to that extent are our own chances of exemplarity improved.

What has been the most rewarding lesson? It is this: individuals, past or present, whom I have rated as exemplars, have thought of themselves as among "human beings in general." Their place in the elite category has been bestowed by others—never self-proclaimed. Indeed, any time any person puts a crown on his own head, he is one to shun intellectually, never to follow or emulate. Unfortunately for him, he has failed to grasp how infinitesimal is his own finite consciousness.

Socrates, reputedly one of the wisest, had this to say: "I know nothing, but I know I know nothing." That great Greek referred to himself as a philosophical midwife; he was a go-between—seeking Truth on the one hand, sharing his findings with fellow seekers on the other. Socrates was aware of a simple and self-evident fact: the more one learns, the larger looms the Unknown.

This point is easy to grasp. Merely visualize in the mind's eye a sheet of black, infinite in dimensions—the Unknown. Now whiten a small circle to represent your awareness, perception, consciousness of, say, a decade ago. Next whiten a greatly enlarged circle to depict your growth during the past ten years. Observe how much more darkness you as a learner are exposed to now than earlier. A good guideline to assess progress: if daily the Unknown is not looming larger, one is not growing.

Many who have delved deeply into any subject, be it philosophy, science, or whatever, are keenly aware of this point. Warren Weaver, a distinguished mathematician, generalized the conclusion reached by many thoughtful scientists:

> As science learns one answer, it is characteristically true that it *learns several new questions.* It is as though science were working in a great forest of ignorance within which... things are clear. . . . But, as that circle becomes larger and larger, the circumference of contact with ignorance also gets longer and longer. Science learns more and more. But there is a sense in which it does not gain; for the volume of the *appreciated but not understood* keeps getting larger. We keep, in science, *getting a more and more sophisticated view of our ignorance.*[1] (Italics mine)

Here we are presented with what, at first blush, is a seeming anomaly, namely, the more one is aware of his ignorance the more is he graced with wisdom. These two progressions are complementary rather than contradictory. They are twin aspects of man's most important earthly purpose: *growth* in awareness, perception, consciousness. As suggested above, when one is growing, he becomes more and more aware of his ignorance and this gain in awareness is, in itself, a gain in wisdom. No better lesson is to be learned in The School of Mankind!

Parenthetically, it should be noted that there are among us always those I would class as "false exemplars"—the political charlatans and others who prescribe life without effort, the know-nothings who promise that they, better than we ourselves, can manage our individual destinies.

These "leaders" are the very opposite of exemplars. They are Pied Pipers who put themselves in the vanguard of this or that mob. According to Emerson, a mob is "a society of bodies voluntarily bereaving themselves of reason."

---

[1]See "The Raw Material," *Manas* (Vol. XXVIII, No. 9, February 26, 1975).

My concern is not with mobs and their flabby disposition to escape from freedom and self-responsibility but, rather, with those individuals who aspire to get ever deeper into life. The human future is with those whose ambition is to achieve in their own lives, as nearly as possible, man's manifest destiny!

Very well! Observe the true exemplars and their ways. These all-too-rare souls have their eyes cast only on their own improvement, not on the reforming of anyone else. As a consequence of their adherence to self-perfection, others who would improve themselves are drawn not only to them but to the light they radiate. To seekers, such enlightenment performs as does a magnet.

However, there are and always have been two grades of people: stagnant and growing. There are individuals who seem to be more enlightened on this or that subject than anyone else. Being further advanced than all others, no more is required of them, or so they mistakenly conclude. Stagnated! In a word, they crown themselves and freeze at the level of their self-professed perfection. They *fail to grow*.

It is growth in awareness, and this alone, which energizes the power of attraction; stagnation at whatever level has no magnetism! It matters not at what level of awareness the growth proceeds, be it from a beginner in The School of Mankind or a Socrates. Why? The one who is learning is graced with ideas—enlightenments—new to him and very likely new, or at least refreshing, to those fortunate enough to share his company.

This is a fascinating phenomenon. Magnetism flows between the seekers and the givers of light, much as a flash of lightning oscillates between positive and negative poles. The current may be generated from either direction—by the teacher whose light is growing brighter, or by the student drawing ever more earnestly from the constant light of a great teacher, perhaps one no longer living. Or, most hopefully, the greatest enlightenment might come as teacher and student grow together.

Many times you and I have said and heard others say, "I now see what you mean." Why not before? Countless reasons range from one party's deafness or disinterest to the other's muteness or monotony. It has been said that repetition is the mother of learning, but this is not necessarily the case. Saying the same thing over and over—the broken record—is folly. But trying to phrase an idea in better and more interesting style has merit not only for the phraser but also for the one who may be trying to "see what you mean." Forever strive for clarity; first in one's mind and then in expressions and actions.

The seeker after the light of truth should search in every nook and cranny, for no person knows beforehand from what source it might beam. When he spots it, he should follow wherever it leads. If we are alert, flashes of truth will be observed emanating from those previously unknown as well as from the acclaimed elite, from sometime opponents as well as from long-time friends of freedom, from babes to grownups. Let us pray with Cardinal Newman: "Lead, Kindly Light, amid the encircling gloom. Lead Thou me on!"

When devotees of the free market, private ownership, limited government way of life are chosen as teachers, let orientation be the teachers' aim. Yes, give some samplings of the few lessons well mastered, point out the lodestar—the ideal—and let the seekers take it from there. The School of Mankind has given me two reasons for this conclusion. First, there is no teacher among all who live who knows all the explanations—even remotely. And, second, only the seekers can find their way. No individual can do it for you or me or anyone else. Each, by the very nature of man, is his own trail blazer.

The School of Mankind! It issues no degrees; there is no tenure. Students and teachers leap-frog one another as they advance. No graduation, only daily commencements! And no semesters or set term of years! The School of Mankind is for life—the good life!

25
THE POINT OF CURE

In the history of man it has been very generally the case, that when evils have grown insufferable, they have touched the point of cure.

—E. H. CHAPIN

The evils of runaway government, with its inevitable inflationary consequence, approach the insufferable stage. People by the millions are becoming concerned; in a word, they are waking up and are now wondering what to do about it. Good! As W. S. Gilbert wrote in *The Mikado,* "Don't let's be downhearted. There's a silver lining to every cloud." The silver lining in our dark cloud is this rising solicitude.

I admire Chapin's "*touched* the point of cure." For, regardless of any understanding that grows out of it, let us never get the notion that wonder by itself is all there is to it. This large-scale wonderment merely touches the point of cure and unless handled properly can easily prove abortive. The silver lining is indeed in our politico-economic cloud, but will we act intelligently enough ever to see it? That's the question.

The key to any success we may experience rests on proper treatment. The treatment I have seen thus far seems inappropriate; it is doing more harm than good, and turning sweet wonder into bitter skepticism and opposition. Unless there is an about-face in tactics or method, that silver lining is but an opportunity lost. True, the anxiety has *touched* the point of cure—no more; the problem is to find the role that each must play if our concern is to reach the level of understanding needed to effect a cure.

Here is the situation as I see it—in graphic form:

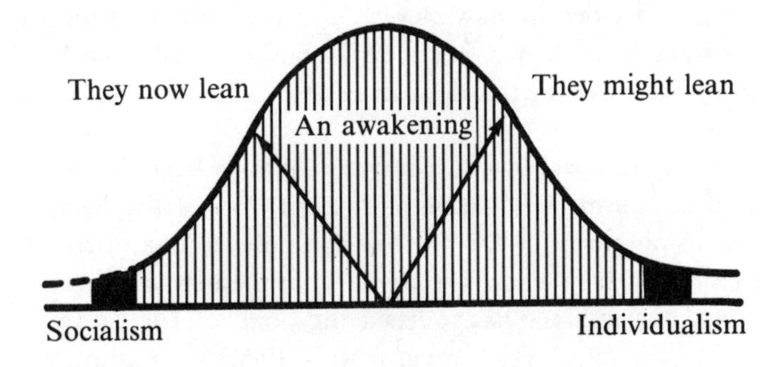

This chart symbolizes adult American society. The segment blocked in at the left represents the very few articulate, persuasive protagonists of socialism. The one at the right represents the small number of free market, private ownership, limited government spokesmen. These on the right are the devotees of the freedom way of life, who partially understand its imperatives and exemplify its essence.

Ranged between these two small polar groups are 130,000,000 adult Americans. While members of this segment may display expertise at a thousand and one specializations, they have few if any ideas—good or bad—when it comes to politico-economic affairs; they merely tend to follow one wing or the other—left or right. The wing they follow will get their votes and, thus, these millions render the final decision as to the political system under which the nation will live.

'Tis a puzzling picture! The millions render the final decision. Yet, which way they lean depends on the byplay between the few thousand in each of the opposing camps. The way the millions go—the fate of the nation—is, in the final analysis, decided by how cleverly the small block at the left conspires to destroy a free society and how profoundly and wisely the block at the right strives to create such a societal ideal.

During the past few decades, the millions have leaned toward socialism. The reason as I see it? We of the freedom persuasion have, for the most part, employed unattractive—even repelling—tactics. The hope? That the new wonderment among the millions has touched the point of cure. Can we achieve the cure? Yes, *provided* we sufficiently improve our understanding and set our tactics straight!

Now for some analysis of ourselves—the block at the right. Opposed to socialism, yes. The remedy? Ever so many among us believe it consists in "selling the masses." This is just as farfetched or unrealistic as selling the multitudes on becoming galactic explorers. Heightened consciousness—knowledge, wisdom, awareness, perception—cannot be sold. Like any other virtue, awareness is a personal acquisition, a quality sought for. I can no more insinuate an idea into your mind than you can ram a notion into mine. Each individual is in charge of his own doors or perception and he absorbs into his ideas and actions only that which he wishes.

If the selling tactic had no other defect than fruitless effort —spinning one's wheels—we could bemoan the fact and let it go at that. The "hard sell," however, sends the prospective customers away from, not toward, the freedom way of life.

Consider the person who insists on sending this book or that article to every member of Congress, or who writes reams of advice to the President of the United States. In effect, straighten them out! Not a responsive word is heard if "the sell" is from a stranger, one whose counsel is not sought.

Such uninvited "wisdom" lands not in the minds of these governmental agents but in their wastebaskets. Further, the freedom way of life is thereby downgraded in the eyes of the besieged. Add to these incorrect methods the drop-out policy of throwing in the sponge, taking a posture exactly the opposite of what it should be. An example in the morning's mail, the concluding sentence to a despondent letter: "I am discouraged. I am angry. But worse, I am becoming apathetic." Since he can't reform others to his taste, he concludes that the case is hopeless; he is not attending to his own practice of freedom.

If someone in high political office—the President or a Congressman—were to seek your counsel, there would be a listening ear, that is, a wanting-to-know-ness coupled with his acknowledgment of you as a fruitful source. If one wishes to be effective, here is a good rule to follow. Wait for the call—the seeking of counsel—but do everything within one's power to qualify for the call.

We must, however, analyze the kind of personal behavior which accounts for such calls. This above all: *seek not agreement* any more than praise; seek only righteousness, pursue only excellence. If this be one's major aim, and if a modicum of progress is made, some of those few among the Remnant—the ones who really count—will find you out. You couldn't hide your light under a bushel if you tried! Light mysteriously shines through, regardless!

The Remnant: In every society there are persons who have the intelligence to figure out the requirements of liberty and the character to walk in its ways. This is a scattered fellowship of individuals—mostly unknown to you or me—bound together by a love of ideas and a hunger to know the plain truth of things. These persons resist the hard sell, or any other kind of sell; they refuse to be fetched. Any suspicion that they might be the target of someone's efforts and they vanish. There is only one way to go about it: Let each cultivate his own garden—pursue excellence—and if he produces anything worthwhile, he may be sure, as Albert Jay Nock says, "that the Remnant will find him. He may rely on that with absolute assurance. They will find him without his doing anything about it; in fact, if he tries to do anything about it, he is pretty sure to put them off. . . ."[1]

Why so much emphasis on the pursuit of excellence as the sole formula for the cure we seek? It stems from this observation: The higher grade the objective, the higher grade must the method be. If one's objective be the destruction of a free

[1]It was forty years ago that I read Nock's "Isaiah's Job" in the *Atlantic Monthly.* Immediately, I quit being a reformer or a name-caller. Mr. Nock not only understood this ancient wisdom recorded in the Old Testament but he did such a brilliant rewriting of it that it caused me and many others to do an about-face. See *Essays on Liberty,* Vol. II, pp. 51-61.

society, low-grade methods suffice. If, on the other hand, the objective be the creation of a free society, then this is as high grade in the politico-economic hierarchy of values as one can go; it correlates with understanding and wisdom and, by the same token, the method must be commensurately as high.

What is this method? It is as simple to state as it is difficult to achieve: *arrive at that excellence in understanding and exposition that will cause others—those who care to know—to seek one's tutorship.* Proof that this works? Merely reflect on those to whom you turn for tutorship in any field of endeavor. Obviously, only to those who, in your judgment, are more, not less, enlightened. For example, golfers at my Club do not seek my tutorship on how to play the game; they are aware of my incompetence. But wave a magic wand and make a Jack Nicklaus of me, and every member will sit at my feet, drink at my fountain, seek my tutorship. This is true in any field one wishes to examine, and in none is it more evident than in the rebirth of liberty—the goal of our ambition.

Yes, we have *touched* the point of cure. A brand new wonderment among 130,000,000 adult Americans awaits only an attracting excellence to *effect* the cure, namely, an about-face from democratic despotism to human liberty. We have ample demonstration that the "hard sell" does not work. So, let's try the learning and sharing process. As Nock said, "We may rely on that with absolute assurance."

26

RIGHT NOW!

By the streets of "by and by" one arrives at the house of "never."

—CERVANTES

By "right now" I mean today; I mean, stand for and proclaim the right as one sees it, not by and by, not tomorrow, but *now!* Truth deferred is truth interred—laid to rest. It has been suggested that he who postpones the honesty of today till tomorrow will probably relegate his tomorrow to eternity. Righteousness can never be born in procrastination but only in the here and now—right now!

What has this to do with human liberty, that is, with the free market, private ownership, limited government way of life? Far more than meets the eye! Perhaps we can respond with a cue from Mark Twain, "Always do right. This will gratify some people and astonish the rest." Doing the right thing these days is so uncommon as to shock most people. Yet, the case for liberty rests on the presumption that a person will behave promptly and voluntarily as righteously as he knows how. A large percentage of the individuals who do perceive the desirability of liberty have two fears: (1) the fear of the unpopularity which attends those who shock their contemporaries and (2) the fear that if what's right were to take place all at once the economy would tumble into a shambles.

A commentary on the first fear: Thirty years ago I was discussing our economic problems with one of the nation's distinguished editors. He saw things clearly. The journal over which he presided was published by one of our leading business organizations. He said to me, "Someone, sometime, must write the truth about our economic dilemma—must explain the only real way out of it."

"Why don't you do it?" asked I.

His reply, "Our organization would be pilloried and ruined."

This man, like many others, thought it dangerous to be openly honest. Further, he regarded his organization as more important than his own honesty. In reality, it was not important that his organization be popular, or even that it survive. It was only important that he and the organization be forthright in the presentation of honest convictions.

The explanations my editor friend expressed privately to me were splendid. Indeed, his words were what most thinking Americans—lovers of liberty—would like to speak and write. Yet, like this editor, they hold their tongues and still their pens for fear that their words might be astonishing, shocking, unpopular.

This poses some serious questions as to how we should order our lives: Why should you or I seek popularity? Is it actually dangerous to be honest? And supposing it were, for what greater cause than individual liberty could risks be taken?

Reflect on the editor's stand, or lack of it, rather. Thirty years ago he was afraid to say what he believed to be right. Yet, there has not been any time since then when the case for liberty could have been made with less astonishment, shock, unpopularity! Indeed, the obstacles and difficulty of gaining a hearing for liberty have mounted steadily year after year. On his own premises, the editor, and those like him, would have remained permanently muted; liberty could have had no spokesman—and all for the shameful fear of being honest. I repeat, truth deferred is truth interred; liberty relegated to the house of "never"!

Now for a commentary on the second fear: that were we devotees of liberty to get our way all at once—the right *suddenly* to replace the wrong—the economy would tumble into a shambles. This fear accounts for "gradualism," the notion that what's right must be implemented slowly and step by step. This, I submit, is a demonstrable fallacy and, if pursued, would and must have the same disastrous results as the other fear: the house of "never"!

It was April 1946. Wartime wage and price controls were still in effect. My lecture, "I'd Push the Button," was delivered in Detroit before the Annual Meeting of the Controllers Institute of America. The title was taken from my opening sentence: "If there were a button on this rostrum, the pressing of which would remove all wage and price controls instantaneously, I would put my finger on it and push." The very opposite of "gradualism"!

Here is an analogy. A big, burly ruffian has me on my back, his knee in my midriff, his hands around my neck. A dozen friends, in typical fashion, are circling the scene, bemoaning the plight of poor, old Read. I can hear their chatter. "We must remove that ruffian, but we must do it gradually or Read will get up and go to work all of a sudden."

There are proofs galore that my analogy is not fantasy. Three outstanding examples may suffice to make the point.

The National Industrial Recovery Act—NRA or The Blue Eagle—became law during the early days of the New Deal. Top business leaders and their national organizations endorsed this fantastic set of government controls over the economy. Why this anti-free market position? For more reasons than I shall ever know, but one was the hope of being rid of dreaded competition. However, after a year or two of these strangling controls, the business leaders and their organizations reversed their position. Abbreviated, their "reasoning" was this: "We must be rid of this political monster, but the riddance must be gradual. To be rid of it suddenly would wreck the economy."

Came May 1935 and the Supreme Court's famous "Chicken Case" decision. As of that moment every phase of NRA was abolished, not an iota of it remained. The wrong abolished suddenly! Did the economy go smash? To the contrary, citizens went suddenly to work. Have a look at the indices—on the up!

Here is the second example. Not being present, I do not know the exact phrasing, but the gist of it was as follows:

An aide to President Truman announced, "Mr. President, the Japanese have surrendered."

"Cancel the war contracts!"

"Why, Mr. President, they amount to $45,000,000,000. That would ruin the economy."

Responded the Commander-in-Chief: "Cancel the war contracts!"

Within hours, telegrams were sent from Washington ordering all contractors to stop right where they were. Economic pandemonium? To the contrary, production for the market took over as the manufacture of war material ceased—suddenly! Look at the indices—on the up!

The third example is the most impressive of all. I was present when it was born: April 1947, at the first meeting of The Mont Pelerin Society. The initiator was Professor Ludwig von Mises.

First, take stock of Mises and his ways. I can speak with authority on this point for he was an intimate acquaintance of mine for thirty three years. Never once did I know him to equivocate. Always, he spoke and wrote what he believed to be right—no heed whatsoever to the approval of anyone. Nor did he push his views; he merely stated and explained them.[1]

Anyway, at this meeting in Switzerland he gave an impressive summary of his politico-economic views—the Austrian School philosophy. Mises presented what he believed to be right—right now. Later, I overheard Professor Wilhelm Roepke, one of the most notable among the founders, vigorously express his disapproval of Mises' views. Two years later, I was invited to dine with Professor and Mrs. Mises, that they "had a guest from Europe." Who did the guest turn out to be? Roepke! In this brief period, Professor Roepke had come to share the views of Mises—philosophically, the two had becoming substantially one.

---

[1]For a good example of Mises and his ways, see "The Individual in Society." Copy on request.

Now for the payoff, the fantastic result of one man's honesty. The Allied Command in Germany imposed all sorts of controls—the Keynesian type of notions. They chose Dr. Ludwig Erhard as their German economic advisor, doubtless because he had degrees in economics and was a noted anti-Nazi. Much to everyone's surprise, Dr. Erhard went on a nationwide radio broadcast one Sunday evening and announced, "Beginning tomorrow morning all wage, price, and other controls are off!"

Dr. Erhard was summoned before the planners of the Allied Command and informed that he could go to prison for such an unauthorized act. "You have modified our controls."

Replied Erhard, "I haven't modified your controls; I have abolished them!"

Dr. Erhard then had to appear before General Clay, the Allied Commander. Said the General, in effect, "Ludwig, I don't know up from down when it comes to economics, but I like you, and I am going to back you."

Witness what happened: the miraculous recovery of a devastated country within a few years, the greatest demonstration of how freedom works its wonders in the Twentieth Century!

The above, however, is the story but not the key to it. The key? Dr. Erhard in one of his books acknowledged that his principal mentor and advisor was Wilhelm Roepke! Observe on what a slender thread the recovery of West Germany was strung: Mises, saying what's right—right now; Roepke coming to share the great man's understanding; and Erhard courageously putting it all into effect.

That West Germany is on the skids again, as is the U.S.A.,

and every other country, can be explained by the absence of such exemplary understanding, honesty, courage.

Said Henry Clay: "I would rather be right than be president." Anyone of that moral mien can have my vote for good citizenship, the head of a household, or company, or country. Without such persons, liberty is out of the question; and without liberty, achieving individual potentialities is out of the question. Thus, give America more of those who will do the right as they see the right—*right now!*

INDEX

Prepared by Vernelia A. Crawford

The letter "n" following a figure refers to a footnote.

H

I

J

K

L

M

N

O

P

R

W